# ENGLISH GARDENS
## OPEN TO THE PUBLIC

THE WATER LILY POOL AT JULIANS, BUNTINGFORD, HERTFORDSHIRE.

A. G. L. HELLYER, FLS

# English Gardens

## OPEN TO THE PUBLIC

COUNTRY LIFE LIMITED

*First published in 1956*
*by Country Life Limited*
*Tavistock Street London WC2*
*Printed in Great Britain by*
*The Shenval Press*
*London Hertford and Harlow*

# Foreword

In preparing a companion volume of Mr Christopher Hussey's *English Country Houses Open to the Public* I have had to follow a somewhat different policy. All the houses which he illustrates and briefly describes are more or less permanently open, many of them, in fact, being in some form of public ownership. Had I similarly restricted myself I should have had to ignore some of the loveliest and most famous gardens in the country, despite the fact that they are frequently opened to the public by the generosity of their owners. Yet to go to the other extreme and attempt to include all those gardens that are opened, perhaps for no more than one or two days in a year, for some charitable purpose, would be an impossible task. I have, therefore, chosen a middle course and have made a selection of what I believe to be some of the most interesting gardens, the majority of which are privately owned and all of which, to the best of my knowledge at the time of writing, are open to the public on some days each year. But those days will necessarily vary from one year to another and it may well be that, through changes of ownership or of circumstance, a time will come when some will be withdrawn from the list altogether. A great many of the gardens are opened for the Queen's Institute of District Nurses or for the Gardeners' Royal Benevolent Institution, and I certainly advise prospective visitors to obtain the lists of both these organizations. The address of the Queen's Institute is 57 Lower Belgrave Street, London, SW1, and of the G.R.B.I., 92 Victoria Street, London, SW1. Other lists of properties are *Country Houses Open to the Public* (Country Life), *Ancient Monuments Open to the Public* (Country Life) and *Historic Houses and Castles in Great Britain Open to the Public* (Index Publishers). All these are revised periodically so that they give the latest information regarding dates and times of opening and charges for admission.

My selection has been limited by the economics of book production and the desire to produce an attractive volume at a popular price. I therefore apologize to all those owners whose gardens, though beautiful and open to the public, are not included in these pages. At the same time I would like to say how pleased I shall be to receive particulars of such gardens, for it may well be that there are some which should be included in any revision of this book.

The gardens I have included cover a very wide range of styles from the severe formality of Kingston Russell to the almost jungle-like profusion of Leonardslee. There are very old gardens such as that at Thornbury Castle as well as comparatively young gardens such as Talbot Manor and Julians. But garden making is a long term process and so the very newest gardens must inevitably be excluded until they have had time to grow up and give some indication of their true merit.

*Rowfant*, 1956                                                                                    A. G. L. HELLYER

# Contents

# CONTENTS

## ACKNOWLEDGEMENTS TO PHOTOGRAPHERS

The photographs are the copyright of either *Country Life* or *Amateur Gardening* with the exception of: Plates 10, 11, Humphrey and Vera Joel; 36, 'Kay'; 61, John Robinson; 71, Tella; 102, Quentin Lloyd; 149, 150, 160, National Trust; 162, Aero Pictorial Ltd; 168, 169, William Whitaker; 172, 173, *Birmingham Post and Mail*; 230, J. E. Downward; 231, Cecil Beaton.

# English Gardens Open to the Public

**1. ABBOTSWOOD: THE FORMAL GARDEN ON THE TERRACE BELOW THE HOUSE**

**Abbotswood, Stow-on-the-Wold, Gloucestershire.** This is a pleasant manor house built of grey Cotswold limestone and largely redesigned early in the twentieth century by Sir Edwin Lutyens. The garden was begun at about the same time by Mr Mark Fenwick, and is an excellent example of those principles of 'natural' gardening which were then being so powerfully advocated by William Robinson and Gertrude Jekyll.

There are skilfully planned herbaceous borders in which the plants have been carefully associated for colour harmony and continuity; shrubs and trees are used plentifully in natural groupings or as isolated specimens; there is an extensive heather garden well sited on the hillside beyond the house and good use has also been made of this hill to construct a long rock garden with central stream cascading swiftly to a pool surrounded by moisture loving plants.

Near the house the garden is terraced in several broad sweeps and the whole treatment is much more formal, but it is a formality which is softened by generous planting, not only of numerous beds and borders cut in the terraces, but also of the retaining walls themselves. The terraces are so designed and planted that they in no way obstruct the view from the house across the surrounding countryside, but rather carry the eye towards it.

Ornamental tree and shrub groupings on the hillside above the terraces gradually merge into the natural coppice of beech and other native trees with which the hill is crowned. Particular attention has been paid to trees and shrubs with coloured foliage and to those that colour or fruit well in the autumn.

Because of its many different features this is a garden which retains interest throughout the year. It is also notable for its deliberate and effective contrast of formal and informal features. There is probably no better preserved example in England today of this particular style of planting.

9

**2. ABBOTSWOOD: ONE OF THE TERRACES BELOW THE HOUSE**

**3. ABBOTSWOOD: STREAM AND ROCK GARDEN IN WOODLAND SETTING**

## 4. ASCOTT: THE DUTCH GARDEN

**Ascott, Wing, Buckinghamshire.** The house is long and half timbered and parts of it are genuinely old, though much was added by Mr Leopold de Rothschild in the last quarter of the nineteenth century. It is situated on high ground with magnificent views across the Vale of Aylesbury and full advantage has been taken of these natural advantages when planning the garden. In the main this consists of a series of walled terraces falling away from the house so that the view is unobstructed. Advantage has been taken of the shelter provided by one of these terraces to grow many plants that are a little tender and this part of the garden is known as the Madeira Walk. In complete contrast to these formal features of Ascott is the extensive lake formed and planted as naturally as possible and surrounded by equally informal plantings of trees and shrubs. Water lilies are used freely in the lake and in summer these provide one of the principal attractions of the garden. In the spring, in addition to the many bright bedding plants, such as wallflowers and tulips, used on the terraces, there are considerable plantings of ornamental cherries which make a spectacular display. An interesting feature of Ascott is the extensive use made of shrubs and trees with variegated foliage.

## 5. ASCOTT: THE POOL ON ONE OF THE TERRACES

6. ASHFORD CHACE: PART OF THE OLD MANOR WHICH HAS BEEN CONVERTED INTO A GARDEN ROOM AND STORE

7. ASHFORD CHACE: THE SMALL SUNKEN GARDEN IN ITALIAN STYLE WHICH WAS DESIGNED BY THE ARCHITECT OF THE HOUSE AS PART OF THE ORIGINAL PLANNING

8. ASHFORD CHACE: THE LONG VISTA FROM THE HOUSE ALONG THE LIP OF THE VALLEY WITH BEECH COVERED HILLS IN THE BACKGROUND

**9. ASHFORD CHACE: ONE OF THE PONDS IN THE VALLEY WITH ASTILBES IN FOREGROUND**

**Ashford Chace, Petersfield, Hampshire.** The garden is long and narrow, situated partly in a shallow valley at the foot of steep, beech-covered hills, and partly along the west lip of the valley, on which the house itself stands. Full use has been made of this natural situation to create a series of vistas hemmed in by groupings of ornamental trees and shrubs, with the hills as a background. A long grass path centred on the house forms the main axis of design and gradually tapers to a flagged path, a scheme which tends to accentuate the length of the garden which has thus been made a virtue rather than a fault. The valley planting is chiefly of interest because of the good use made of tree colour in which acers, cherries, cerci-diphyllums and willows play a prominent part. At the far end of the garden beneath the hills are the remnants of an old manor house part of which has been preserved to provide a summer house around which what is almost a separate garden has been created consisting of a lawn, large pool planted with water lilies and surrounded by moisture-loving plants, and groupings of trees and shrubs, notably magnolias and gingkos. The most formal feature is a small, sunken garden on the east side of the house. This has markedly Spanish features in harmony with a similar trend in the architectural treatment of the terrace and house front on this side. It was, in fact, designed by the architect to complete the effect he desired.

**10. BARNWELL MANOR: THE FORMAL TERRACES NEAR THE HOUSE**

**Barnwell Manor, Peterborough, North-amptonshire.** An outstanding feature of this garden is the ruined thirteenth century castle which is situated to the west of the manor. On the crumbling walls of this castle there are great drifts of aubrieta, pink valerian, perennial wallflowers and other flowers. Between castle and manor is a formal water lily pool. The manor house is surrounded by extensive lawns. Well trimmed yew hedges on the east side give an added firmness to the design. The terrace around the house is paved and balustraded in stone and a great many creeping plants such as thymes, sedums and saxifrages have been established in the crevices between the paving slabs. Large drifts of daffodils and crocuses are naturalised in grass as well as other spring bulbs. Good shrubberies, planted in the modern manner, as well as many specimen shrubs and trees, add to the variety of the scene.

**11. BARNWELL MANOR: THE LILY POOL AND RUINED CASTLE**

**12. BARRINGTON COURT: BORDERS FILLED WITH DAHLIAS AND OTHER LATE SUMMER FLOWERS**

**Barrington Court, Ilminster, Somerset.** There are two linked houses at Barrington Court, both dating back to Tudor times but one a residence from the outset and the other, until recent years, a stable block. The first is built of stone and is a highly romantic and very beautiful building which has been left to make its effect without any impedimenta of plants. Garden making, as distinct from the laying of lawns and the planting of a few specimen trees, has been confined to the area around the converted stable block, a rather stolid brick building which is all the better for the competing colour of flowers. And a very colourful garden this is, especially the great walled rectangle to the south of the build-ing, with its central lily pool, raised beds of brilliant annuals and crinums and surrounding borders packed with herbaceous plants and shrubs. Flanking this main garden are two more, one wholly enclosed and devoted to roses, the other more open and mainly filled with beds of irises. There are other interest-ing features in this garden, notably the long borders filled in summer with dahlias, the splendid herbaceous borders shel-tered by the kitchen garden wall, and the modern style shrub garden with wide grass walks winding between beds of irregu-lar shape and ample size. Considered as a whole this is a garden of exceptionally rich and colourful planting to be seen at its best in summer.

**13. BARRINGTON COURT: RAISED BEDS SURROUNDING THE OVAL POOL IN THE WALLED GARDEN**

**14. BARRINGTON COURT: THE WALLED GARDEN AS SEEN FROM THE HOUSE**

## 15. BATEMANS: THE ROSE GARDEN, POOL AND PLEACHED LIMES

**Batemans, Burwash, Sussex.** This lovely old Jacobean house was for many years the
home of Rudyard Kipling and is now preserved by the National Trust exactly as it was
when Kipling lived there. This applies as
much to the garden as to the house itself, and
it is fortunate that this is a garden that can be
preserved in such a way without suffering in
the process. It is a simple yet dignified
garden, relying for its effect more on fine proportions, good lawns and trained trees than
upon the multitude of plants that tend to in-
vade the average twentieth century garden.
Good use has been made of the natural contours of the land to plan a garden on several
levels, with old Sussex sandstone retaining
walls matching the grey stone of the building
itself. A prominent and essential feature is a
large rectangular pool. At one end are rose
beds which provide a touch of bright colour.
Two fine rows of skilfully pleached limes are
centred on the south side of the house.

## 16. BATEMANS: THE RESTRAINED PLANTING AROUND THE HOUSE

**17. BAYFORDBURY: ONE OF THE GLASS CORRIDORS PERMANENTLY PLANTED**

**Bayfordbury, Hertford, Hertfordshire.** Like so many fine mansions of the eighteenth and early nineteenth century, Bayfordbury has proved too large and too costly for private ownership and has passed into public hands. It is fortunate that its present owners, the governors of the John Innes Horticultural Institution, are as interested in gardening as any of the wealthy gentlemen who inhabited it for nearly 200 years. Since Bayfordbury was acquired as a research station some changes have inevitably been made in the garden but many of these have actually added to its variety, interest and beauty.

The original garden followed the rather severe landscape style still fashionable in the early nineteenth century. A large lawn, unhampered by beds, sweeps almost to the house, to right and left of which are groups of fine trees including many

good conifers, some of which date back to about 1760. Beyond the south-west wing was a formal rose garden and further removed from the house on this same side, a fine natural lake. Both these features remain but the rose garden is now filled with old and historic varieties and an entirely new garden which presents a genealogical picture of the development of the garden races of rose from the wild species has been planted nearby.

The National Collection of Rose Species has been accommodated in a series of large beds well sited on rising ground, between the mansion and the new glasshouses. These glasshouses, which are essential to the work of the Institution, have been linked by wide corridors which are themselves permanently planted with an exceptionally fine collection of tender plants.

**18. BEECHWOOD: THE LAWN AND SHRUB BEDS FRAMING THE UNEXPECTEDLY FINE VIEW**

**Beechwood, Highgate, Middlesex.** In common with Lady Crosfield's remarkable garden at 41 Highgate West Hill, Beechwood enjoys the advantage of that extraordinary rural intrusion into northern London which is, in fact, a remnant of the ancient Forest of Middlesex and has marvellously retained much of its original character. In this delightful setting a garden has been made which really deserves to be described as 'landscape'. It is entirely informal and relies mainly upon fine sweeps of lawn broken by bold groupings of shrubs and many fine trees.

To the west there is a small valley, the apparent depth and importance of which have been cunningly increased by planting many tall trees on its further side. A stream flows through it but this, despite its natural appearance, is a clever contrivance of the landscape artist, the water being pumped back from a small lake which terminates it.

Daffodils and crocuses have been naturalised freely in the grass around the house and elsewhere. The large beech trees, which are a legacy from the Forest of Middlesex, add greatly to the beauty and dignity of this garden and modern plantings include such fine exotic trees as the cork oak and the swamp cypress.

In its emphasis upon landscape and its restrained use of plants as elements of design rather than as ends in themselves, this modern garden derives directly from the great gardens of the mid eighteenth century.

It is a rare pleasure to find so fine an example of landscape planting so close to London and one may hope that no development schemes are permitted to encroach upon it or its unique view.

### 19. BINGHAM'S MELCOMBE: THE BOWLING GREEN AND YEW HEDGE

**Bingham's Melcombe, Dorchester, Dorset.**
This is a garden in which one can well imagine that
time has stood still. There is an illustration by Joseph
Nash, more than 100 years old, that shows the pleasantly enclosed forecourt with its stone terrace wall
surmounted by fine hydrangeas almost exactly as it is
today. The walls of the terrace and surrounding buildings are now more heavily clothed with plants but not
so much as to screen the beauty of the Tudor oriole
which dominates this courtyard.

The main garden is a bowling green screened by an
immense yew hedge beyond which is a vegetable
garden designed for ornament as well as utility and in
which provision has been made for flower borders as
well as for fruit trees and vegetables. The yew hedge,
which rises like a rampart, is one of the glories of
Bingham's Melcombe. The grass sweeps cleanly to
its base without any unnecessary detail to detract
from its impressive stature. The bowling green is terminated by an alcove or garden room in old brick and
the vegetable garden also has an architectural feature
in a fine circular dove-cote at its east end. Beyond the
vegetable garden well-grown limes, sycamores and firs
give shelter and lead on naturally to a wild garden in
which there is a stream and some very old fishponds.

### 20. BINGHAM'S MELCOMBE: THE EN-CLOSED FORECOURT WITH ITS RAISED TERRACE

**21. BLENHEIM PALACE: THE PARTERRE TO THE SOUTH EAST OF THE HOUSE**

**Blenheim Palace, Woodstock, Oxfordshire.** The garden at Blenheim Palace as it is today is the result of three separate periods of planning. The first occurred when the palace was built in the early eighteenth century, when its architect, Sir John Vanbrugh, and its first gardener, Henry Wise, designed a garden which was severely formal and which led the eye, in the fashion of the day, to a great vista enclosed by ranks of elms.

The elaborate parterres and courts around the house disappeared fifty years later when 'Capability' Brown redesigned the gardens in the landscape style. He made the great lake which is now a main feature of the park, but he also brought his broad sweep of grass right up to the walls of the palace, thus leaving it in an isolation which its designer had certainly not intended and which ill-befitted its rather elaborate design.

The ninth Duke of Marlborough, aware of this incongruity and assisted by a French architect, Achille Duchene, succeeded in keeping the best features of 'Capability' Brown's garden and yet giving the palace a suitably dignified and formal setting. This they did first by restoring the Great Court to the north of the house; then by re-making the formal garden to the south-east of the house, both tasks being completed between the years 1900 and 1910 and finally, in 1925, by making an entirely new formal water terrace to the south-west of the house which linked it in an entirely satisfactory way with 'Capability' Brown's informal lake beyond.

These formal gardens restore the Palace to its proper setting. They are on a scale and of an originality that has seldom, if ever, been equalled in the twentieth century and they rival, in their complexity, the original parterres of Vanbrugh and Wise.

**22. BLENHEIM PALACE: THE INFORMAL LAKE MADE BY 'CAPABILITY' BROWN**

**23. BLENHEIM PALACE: THE FORMAL WATER GARDENS WHICH LINK THE HOUSE TO THE LAKE**

### 24. BLICKLING HALL: RECTANGULAR HERBACEOUS BEDS AND TOPIARY ON THE LAWN

**Blickling Hall, Aylsham, Norfolk.** This famous Norfolk house dates back to the early seventeenth century when it was designed by Robert Lyminge for Sir Henry Hobart. The garden is of eighteenth-century conception and was originally laid out with elaborate formal beds and grass lawns around the house, leading by way of fine flights of stone steps to a tree-bordered grass avenue, terminated by a substantial stone temple. Other radiating avenues were cut through these trees to converge diagonally on this temple, so providing those formal vistas beloved of the eighteenth-century garden designer. In order to cope with the more economical requirements of twentieth-century gardening the formal bedding features at Blickling Hall were drastically re-designed early in the present century. The beds were reduced in number and greatly simplified in design and were planted permanently with herbaceous perennials, thus providing one of the most notable examples in England of plants of this character used in a formal way. The treatment of the planting throughout is firm and architectural, and entirely in keeping with the character of the Tudor building. Other features have been retained unaltered but the planting of walls and terraces has been enriched with many exotic shrubs and climbers.

### 25. BLICKLING HALL: THE TEMPLE AT THE FAR END OF THE WOODLAND AVENUE

**26. BLICKLING HALL: LOOKING BACK TO THE HOUSE FROM THE WOODLAND**

**27. BODNANT: THE VIEW FROM THE HOUSE ACROSS THE TERRACES AND THE RIVER CONWAY**

**28. BODNANT: THE LAWN
NEAR THE HOUSE**

**Bodnant, Tal-y-Cafn, Denbighshire.**
The garden as it exists today is very
much the work of the first Lord Aberconway who began to make the great
terraces about 1905. He did, however,
design within the framework of fine
trees already provided by his mother,
herself a keen gardener. Bodnant is
famous for its magnificent views across
the Conway Valley to Snowdonia, its
wonderfully rich collection of plants
and its varied features of design, rang-
ing from the five great terraces which
fall like giant steps before the house,
to the woodland planting of the valley
below which becomes progressively
wilder towards its head. The terraces
are interesting architecturally because
each is different in depth, width and design and yet all have been given a sense
of unity, in part by the similarity of the
material used in their construction—a
local stone—and in part by the plants

**29. BODNANT: THE CANAL
TERRACE AND PIN MILL**

**30. BODNANT: THE LARGE
WATER-LILY POOL ON THE
THIRD TERRACE**

with which they are furnished. These
are mainly shrubs with some herbaceous plants, particularly on the
lowest terrace, water lilies on this and
the third terrace and a rose garden on
the fourth terrace. The bottom terrace,
though farthest removed from the house,
is the most formal in conception. Its
central feature is a long, severely rectangular canal pool. At one end is a
garden house known as the Pin Mill,
an early eighteenth-century Cotswold
building brought to Bodnant piecemeal
in 1938 and re-erected there. At the
other end of this terrace is a fine open air
stage with wings formed of clipped yews.

Lord Aberconway was particularly
interested in rhododendrons and bred
many new varieties. In the valley there
are many fine conifers as well as broad-
leaved trees and a great variety of
shrubs.

**31. BODNANT: THE OPEN-AIR
STAGE**

**32. BORDE HILL: NATURALISED BULBS, RHODODENDRONS AND OTHER SHRUBS**

**33. BRAMHAM: THE T-SHAPED CANAL SURROUNDED BY LARGE TREES**

**Borde Hill, Haywards Heath, Sussex.** This is one of the many notable gardens that have been made on the forest soil of Sussex, though it lies a little to the south of the main ridge of this soil which extends roughly from Hastings to Horsham. Borde Hill stands on a low hill of its own with good views, mainly to the north. Considering the aspect and its comparatively low altitude, it contains a surprisingly wide selection of the more tender shrubs including such fine Cornish bred rhododendrons as Penjerrick and Cornish Cross. The garden was mainly planted by Col Stevenson Clark during the years immediately succeeding the first world war. With the exception of a small enclosed garden between the house and the kitchen garden, it is almost entirely informal in conception with lawns surrounded by woodland which is itself generously underplanted with rhododendrons and other shrubs. On the sloping ground to the north of the house, shrubs and rhododendrons are again used but in beds separated by winding grass paths. A stone balustraded terrace above this planting commands an uninterrupted view of the countryside over the top of the shrubs. Borde Hill provides a good example of the informal style of semi-woodland planting which was so typical an aspect of garden making during the years between the two world wars.

**Bramham Park, Boston Spa, Yorkshire.** The house at Bramham, built during the reign of Queen Anne, is strongly influenced by the Italian school in architecture, and it is fitting that the garden which surrounds it should also be reminiscent of the great continental gardens of that period, designed by Le Nôtre and those who followed his precepts. It is a garden which relies greatly on long vistas created by planting avenues of clipped beeches. One such avenue, the famous Broad Walk, extends southwards from a formal parterre to the west of the house, carrying the eye to an elaborate series of water basins constructed on different levels. To the north of the parterre are other alleys and, in particular, one of greater size and importance with various architectural features. Most notable of these is a large canal in the form of a T. This is completely surrounded by large trees which increase the sense of calm and seclusion. Everywhere at Bramham trees are used to give this feeling of enclosure, to add to the cloistered effect of the alleys and to extend and contain the vistas. In gardens such as this plants play a subsidiary role, being used, as brick or stone might be, to shape a three-dimensional pattern and to direct the eye to certain chosen points in the landscape. Water is used as a dramatic contrast to the texture of plants and soil.

**34. BRATTLES GRANGE: NATURAL GROUPINGS OF TREES AND SHRUBS**

**Brattles Grange, Brenchley, Kent.** The garden is a fine example of the use of hardy plants, including both herbaceous perennials and shrubs, to provide an informal yet carefully conceived design notable for its texture of leaf, flower and stem as well as for its colour and contour. The term 'organic gardening' has been applied to this kind of planting to obtain effects of mass, light and shade which in other periods would have been produced architecturally. Much of the garden site was originally woodland which was drastically thinned to make room for the varied plant material which has been introduced to it. Wide grass paths separate the various groupings of plants. Roses are used freely, particularly shrub roses such as the hybrid musks and the species.

**35. BRATTLES GRANGE: THE HOUSE FROM THE HEATHER GARDEN**

**36. BURNBY HALL: THE UPPER WATER-LILY LAKE WITH THE HOUSE BEYOND**

**Burnby Hall, Pocklington, Yorkshire.** It is doubtful if there is in the British Isles any other purely artificial water-lily garden on the scale of that at Burnby Hall. Here two concreted lakes have been built covering, together, more than two acres. They are at different levels, Upper Water, which is 205 yards long and 70 yards wide, being about 10 feet above Lower Water which is 110 yards long and 30 yards wide. Constructional work was carried out between 1903 and 1910 and it is said that £8,000 was spent on the work. Today the appearance of these two fine lakes, with their hundreds of water lilies and generous marginal planting, is so natural that it is difficult to believe that they are, in fact, entirely the work of man. The rural setting helps this illusion for the village cricket pitch comes down to the edge of the lower lake and beyond the Upper Water the tower of Pocklington Church can be seen.

The varieties of water-lily have been arranged with great care for colour effect and they range from pure white, cream and blush pink to deep yellow and crimson. In all there are nearly sixty different varieties of water-lily at Burnby Hall, and many more have been tried but rejected as unsuitable for the situation. Only those remain which do well in the rather cold Yorkshire climate and which flower freely every year. In consequence the summer spectacle of water-lilies in bloom at Burnby Hall is one that never fails to attract a great number of visitors.

## 37. BUSCOT PARK: THE LONG WALK WITH ITS CENTRAL CANAL

**Buscot Park, Faringdon, Berkshire.** The garden was largely made to the design of Mr Harold Peto early in the present century. Mr Peto was strongly influenced by the classic Italian style, and believed that form was of far more importance than colour or variety of planting material. In pursuance of these ideas he created a long formal walk, quite straight though varying in level, connecting the house with a 20-acre lake which lies on lower ground to the northeast. This walk consists of a chain of stairways, paths and pools with various features of interest which are only revealed as one passes along it. The walk is at first fairly open but soon passes into woodland where it is rather closely enclosed by trees, the sense of confinement being increased by clipped hedges of box and yew. A long narrow canal runs down the centre of this walk, linking a series of formal pools, some with fountains or other ornaments. The whole is flanked by various ornaments in stone—seats, statues and vases carefully displayed against the dark background of foliage. The final vista is across the lake to well-wooded country beyond, the contrast so well loved by all makers of this type of garden between the sophistications of man and the freedom of nature.

## 38. BUSCOT PARK: ONE OF THE MANY FEATURES WHICH DIVERSIFY IT

**39. BUXTED PARK: FORMAL TREAT-
MENT NEAR THE HOUSE**

**Buxted Park, nr Uckfield, Sussex.** The
fine Georgian mansion at Buxted Park was partly
destroyed by fire in 1940 and was later rebuilt in
a modified form with one story less but retaining
much of its original character. The garden which
surrounds this building has remained virtually
unchanged and relies for its effect partly on the
colour provided by massed shrubs, and partly on
extensive vistas, particularly to the east where
the land falls away considerably and gives fine
views across meadows to distant woods. The
planning throughout is on spacious and dignified
lines as befits the building, and is notably free of
fussy details and conceits of all kinds. The vista
to the east is framed by large groupings of
shrubs on one side and by more shrubs giving
way to woodland on the other. This woodland
has also been generously underplanted with
camellias and other shade-loving shrubs, many
of which have grown to great size. There is thus
a reasonable compromise between the demands
of formality imposed by the nature of the building to which this garden provides a setting and
the desire to grow a fairly representative selection
of fine trees and shrubs.

**40. BUXTED PARK: THE FINE VISTA
TO THE EAST**

### 41. CASTLE DROGO: HERBACEOUS BORDERS AND ROSE GARDEN

**Castle Drogo, Drewsteignton, Devonshire.** This remarkable house was built by Sir Edwin Lutyens in the form of a mediaeval castle. It stands on a promontory of land and very properly no gardening has been carried out immediately around it. The garden is on a level terrace completely surrounded by a formal hedge which suggests the battlements of the castle. In the centre is a rather severe rose garden with rectangular beds set in grass and flanked by wide double borders of herbaceous plants at a slightly higher level and unusual in their rather formal design.

At the end of this terrace the ground rises and the garden takes on a much more informal aspect, borders of flowering shrubs leading upwards to two erect cypresses which stand sentinel at the summit of the rise.

### 42. CASTLE DROGO: INFORMAL BORDERS OF FLOWERING SHRUBS

**43. CHARTWELL: THE HOUSE AND TERRACE SEEN FROM THE SOUTH**

**Chartwell, Westerham, Kent.** Famous as the home of Sir Winston Churchill, Chartwell overlooks some of the loveliest country in England. Like so many English manor houses, it has grown with the centuries so that from quite small beginnings in the Tudor style it has become a building of some size. The land slopes sharply to the south-east and the garden has been terraced on this side. At house level a croquet lawn is surrounded by a formal hedge of yew and at a slightly lower level another fine grass terrace is retained by a wall of grey stone. From it there is not only a magnificent view of the countryside but also of the lakes below the house on which the famous black swans live. Colour is chiefly to be found in the walled rose garden, connected by a vine-covered pergola with the Marlborough pavilion at the extreme west end of the terrace. A path from the rose garden leads down through a miniature jungle of bamboos to the fish pond from which water flows over a massive waterfall and down the hillside to a circular swimming pool.

**44. CHARTWELL: THE VALLEY FROM THE WATERFALL WITH THE SWIMMING POOL BELOW**

**45. CHATSWORTH:
FORMAL BEDS
AND AVENUES**

**46. CHATSWORTH:
THE SOUTH
FRONT ON WHICH
IS A LONG CANAL**

## 47. CHATSWORTH: THE GREAT CASCADE WITH THE CASCADE HOUSE IN THE BACKGROUND

**Chatsworth, Bakewell, Derbyshire.** This great garden is the result of making and re-making, alteration and addition over a period of nearly 300 years. Many great names have been connected with it, London and Wise in the late seventeenth century, 'Capability' Brown in the middle of the succeeding century, Sir Jeffrey Wyatville and Sir Joseph Paxton during the first half of the nineteenth century. Not all the changes have been for the better, but nevertheless today Chatsworth can boast a garden which for magnificence of architectural scope and variety of design is second to none in the country.

Immediately around the house the broad sweep of 'Capability' Brown's landscape design has been suitably held back from too close an approach to the mansion by the fine stone terracing introduced by Wyatville. The great cascade on the east side of the house has remained unchanged since 1699, and is a unique and spectacular feature always very popular with visitors. It rushes from an elaborate Cascade House at the summit of a small hill down a great flight of stone steps in a series of miniature waterfalls. Water is used freely in many other parts of the gardens in fountains, pools and canals and there is a curious conceit in the form of a tree made of copper, every branch of which is a fountain.

Around these sophisticated and, in the main, highly architectural features are more natural plantings of trees and shrubs and a great walk of grass starting near the west front of the house takes a circuitous course through this outer garden or arboretum into which rhododendrons and other flowering shrubs have been introduced to give greater variety to the planting and increased colour to the scene. There is, in consequence, something for every taste at Chatsworth yet so large is the scale and so successful the planning that there is no element of incongruity in this rather unusual variety of ingredients.

## 48. CHETWODE MANOR: PATTERNED BEDS OF OLD ROSES AND HERBACEOUS PLANTS

**Chetwode Manor, Preston Bissett, Buckinghamshire.** Roses are the outstanding feature of this garden; not the more formal hybrid tea varieties of most modern gardens, but the old roses which are in danger of being forgotten. Damasks, Bourbons, Gallicas, Moss Roses, Albas, Musks and many others fill the garden with colour and perfume in June and July. They are planted generously and have been allowed to grow into fine bushes with the minimum of pruning or other interference with their natural habit. They are used in a setting that is formal in conception though informal in treatment—a series of squares divided into triangular segments by low lavender hedges and placed in a long rectangle closed in by a hedge of beech on the one side, a wall and pleached limes on the other but open at the end facing the house to the fields and hedgerows beyond. The planting, apart from the roses, is extremely varied and very much in the cottage garden tradition. There is lavender and rosemary, alpine phloxes and lavender cotton, irises, foxgloves, peonies and columbines in a glorious riot of colour and fragrance. The whole is dominated by a large weeping willow and the house front is itself heavily draped with wistaria, roses and other plants.

## 49. CHETWODE MANOR: THE DESIGN MORE CLEARLY REVEALED FROM AN UPPER WINDOW

**50. CHILWORTH MANOR: LAWNS ON SEVERAL LEVELS DIVERSIFIED BY RESTRAINED PLANTING**

**Chilworth Manor, nr Guildford, Surrey.** The garden is remarkable in that the basic design has remained unchanged since the early sixteenth century. To the north of the house the land rises, gently at first and then more steeply, to St Martha's Hill, the lower slopes of which have been cut into three wide terraces separated by stone retaining walls. This part of the garden is enclosed by a high brick wall but a clairvoyée has been left in the north wall centred upon the house and permitting from it a vista of the hillside beyond. The planting is restrained as befits a garden of this classical simplicity, with apple trees emphasising the line of the terraces and Irish yews giving a more dominant accent in the background. Simple stone steps lead from one terrace to another and beds are filled with irises and other homely flowers. The terraces themselves are grassed and the lawn of the lowest terrace continues around the west side of the house to connect the flower garden with a wild garden made around the old stew pond. Beds of simple pattern have been cut in the lawns and are filled with tulips, forget-me-nots and other flowers in season, but no elaborate bedding is attempted nor is it necessary in this setting.

**51. CHILWORTH MANOR: ANOTHER VIEW OF THE HOUSE**

**52. CLARE COLLEGE: THE RIVER WALK WITH THE MAIN GARDEN TO THE LEFT**

**53. CLARE COLLEGE: A MIXED BORDER PLANTED MAINLY WITH WHITE FLOWERS**

**54. CLARE COLLEGE: ONE OF THE HERBACEOUS BORDERS WITH KING'S COLLEGE CHAPEL BEYOND**

**Clare College, Cambridge** At Clare there are, in fact, two quite distinct gardens separated by the River Cam. On the east side of the river are the college buildings and between them and the river bank is a small and simply designed garden with beds of roses and other flowers. This is variously known as the Scholars' Garden or the Master's Garden. The river is crossed here by a lovely stone bridge designed by Thomas Grumbold in 1662, and on the far bank is the Fellows' Garden which is of much greater size and more complex design. It is this garden which is from time to time opened to the public and it is of interest for its excellent planning and planting. The major part of the garden is disposed around a long and irregular lawn backed by fine trees and flanked by wide borders of flowers. Great care has been paid to the colour scheme which is mainly in blue and pink towards the river but becomes increasingly more mixed further back. Right in the foreground, as the garden is viewed from the college or the river, are other beds of red and crimson flowers, the whole colour scheme being intended to increase the appearance of depth in the vista as a whole. To the south are two more wide borders separated by a gravel path. These borders are quite straight and are planted entirely with blue and yellow flowers to give their peak display around midsummer. Concealed by a wall, well clothed with climbing plants, is yet another border in which white flowers predominate. A small sunken garden, enclosed by a yew hedge and with a formal lily pool, provides a place of retreat, and there is also a small garden devoted to fragrant flowers.

**55. CLIVEDEN: THE GREAT TERRACE WHICH PROVIDES A FIRM SETTING FOR THE HOUSE**

**56. CLIVEDEN: THE LAWN AND PARTERRE WITH THE RIVER BEYOND**

**Cliveden, Taplow, Buckinghamshire.** The original plan of the garden is much older than the present house which was designed by Sir Charles Baring in the mid-nineteenth century. Earlier mansions on the site had been rebuilt or destroyed by fire and the first house was built nearly 200 years before the present house was commenced. In consequence the garden has had a long and varied history. Today it is a fine example of formal design, strongly influenced by the Italian school, but gradually modified to meet modern requirements and tastes. There is still the same fine sweep of design, the extensive vistas from house to the river and the surrounding countryside, and the skilful use of ornament to give character and emphasis to the scene. The house itself is displayed upon a great terrace supported by an elaborate stone wall balustraded and buttressed and further ornamented with carvings, statues and other architectural features. This is garden designing on the grand manner and fully in keeping with the majestic view across a great sweep of lawn broken by the formal pattern of box-edged parterres which are still maintained in good order. Only in its more outlying parts does the garden break completely with the traditions of the past and embrace the informality and natural planting of the twentieth century in an extensive water garden well stocked with water lilies and surrounded by a great variety of plants including rhododendrons and other shrubs. There is also an unusual herbaceous border formally enclosed in box.

**57. COLES: THE MAIN VISTA CUT OUT OF A NATURAL WOODLAND**

**Coles, Privett, Hampshire.** This is a comparatively new garden and one which well exemplifies the twentieth-century trend in the natural use of trees and shrubs. The site was well wooded and sufficient of the original trees have been cleared to give a long vista from the house. Further interest has been added to this by bold plantings of flowering shrubs grouped carefully for colour. Grass paths wind through the thin woodland and have been so cleverly disposed that they give an exaggerated impression of the extent of the whole garden. To one side of the main vista a large pool, in form not unlike a dewpond, has been made and a genuine dewpond has been retained on the other side of the house. All this has given scope for a great deal of informal planting in which azaleas and rhododendrons figure prominently. Primulas and other moisture-loving plants are massed in the damp soil around the lakes. Beds are of large size and irregular shape and sufficient large trees have been retained in or near them to give top-cover to shade-loving or slightly tender plants. Formal features are confined to the area near the house where there is a rose garden of simple design and a small flagged garden enclosed by yew hedges and with a central rectangular lily pool.

**58. COLES: PRIMULAS AROUND THE LAKE**      **59. COLES: THE FORMAL GARDEN AND POOL**

**60. COLES: THE HOUSE AS SEEN FROM THE MAIN WOODLAND CLEARING**

**61. COMPTON WYNYATES: GIANT TOPIARY SPECIMENS STAND LIKE CHESSMEN ON THE LAWNS IN FRONT OF THE TUDOR HOUSE**

**Compton Wynyates, Banbury, Warwickshire.** The lovely old house, first built in the twelfth century but largely remodelled in Tudor times, stands in a natural bowl of land almost completely surrounded by grass slopes on which fine trees grow in the typical manner of the English parkland. The garden at one time consisted mainly of a considerable parterre planted with hardy perennials but numerous topiary specimens were placed among these and, with the passage of time, these have grown so large that they now dominate the garden. That, perhaps, is a good thing for not only do these curiously-cut shrubs match the romantic nature of the building and the battlemented hedges of yew which extend from it, but because of their solidity and size they are effective from a distance. And Compton Wynyates can, from its situation, be viewed to great advantage from its surrounding slopes as the accompanying illustration very clearly shows. The basic design is a series of large rectangles with topiary specimens marking the corners and the centre of each, but the shapes into which these shrubs have been clipped are so varied that one is more aware of diversity of form than of uniformity in plan. Standard trees further break up the pattern and add to the strongly three-dimensional effect. The slopes themselves have been kept fairly clear of trees so that there is an uninterrupted view of the garden.

**62. COPPINS: NATURALISED DAFFODILS IN A PARKLAND SETTING**

**Coppins, Iver, Buckinghamshire.** The house is not of any great architectural quality, but it is a pleasant building in a most attractive setting. The garden, which was formerly heavily overplanted with evergreen shrubs in the Victorian manner, was almost entirely remade by H.R.H. the Duke of Kent just before the second World War. He transformed it into a fine example of modern parkland with more intimate features in the form of a sunken garden on the east front, long double herbaceous borders terminated by wrought iron gates and a small garden enclosed by walls which shut it away from the rest as a 'secret' garden.

The extensive and charming parkland, which sweeps away from the house to south and west, has been treated in a spacious manner, the finest or most strategically placed of the old trees having been retained as specimens or in small groups, but the rest have been cleared away to leave ample areas of open grass in which daffodils and other bulbs have been naturalised so that this part of the garden is at its loveliest in the spring.

From the standpoint of planning considerable interest centres in the sunken garden to the east of the house because the narrowness of the site made this difficult to design effectively. The result achieved by paying careful attention to proportion and using comparatively narrow borders in which bedding plants are massed to give maximum colour in small space is in every way satisfactory.

**63. COTEHELE: THE TERRACES BELOW THE HOUSE RETAINED BY STONE WALLS**

**Cotehele, Calstock, Cornwall.** There are really two quite distinct gardens at Cotehele, a formal garden terraced in stone in front of the fine old Tudor house with its massive granite walls, and then, farther afield, a woodland garden in which all idea of formality is abandoned in favour of a natural scheme of planting in which rhododendrons, hydrangeas and other fine shrubs grow freely in the welcome shelter of trees.

The position of the house is a fine one high above the Tamar valley with cliffs dropping sharply to it, and full advantage has been taken of these natural amenities in planning the garden. A small stream flows through this garden and advantage has been taken of the moist ground around it to naturalise primulas and meconopsis which thrive in such places.

Under the National Trust the garden has been planned to keep maintenance costs at a minimum and this has been achieved partly by relying almost exclusively on permanent features such as flowering shrubs and partly by making use of the woodland in which weed growth is, in any case, kept to a minimum by the competition of trees. These are modern ideas in gardening and it is interesting to see at Cotehele how well they fit into an old and historic setting.

More formal features have been retained near the house where there is a simple arrangement of rectangular terraces retained by dry walls, freely planted and with long flower borders cut out of the lawns.

## 64. COTTESBROOK HALL: THE SUNKEN GARDEN LEADING TO THE HERBACEOUS BORDERS

**Cottesbrook Hall, Northampton.** The house is of classical design, built early in the eighteenth century and having a central block linked by curving walls to two smaller buildings or pavilions on either side which partially enclose the forecourt. The garden was largely replanned in the 1930's and at this time the entrance was moved to what had previously been the back of the house, the old forecourt being turfed and brought into the garden scheme with clipped yews and low box hedges. The main garden is to the west of the house. First there is a paved sunk garden with formal beds and lily pool and then, centred on this and running westwards, are long herbaceous borders separated by a flagged path. A low brick wall separates these borders from a formal pool garden notable for its simplicity and the good use made of simple architectural features and, beyond this, is a long grass walk enclosed by yew hedge and brick wall, leading to the wilder and outlying parts. Good planning is the keynote of this garden in which both architectural features and plants have been used with discretion to further the design rather than for their own sake.

## 65. COTTESBROOK HALL: THE GRASS WALK BETWEEN WALL AND HEDGE

**66. CRANBORNE: A BIRD'S EYE VIEW OF THE GARDEN SHOWING THE ELABORATE ENCLOSURE**

**Cranborne, Cranborne, Dorset.** There are few lovelier manor houses in England than Cranborne, which was built in the early seventeenth century and shows markedly the influence of the Italian style. The garden was designed at the same time as the house and, though it has since been much altered in detail and in planting, it still remains unchanged in general conception. It is, as one would expect, largely a walled garden with clipped hedges to supplement the sense of enclosure so dear to the garden designer of that day. In former days the entrance was to the lovely loggia on the north front of the building but this arrangement has now been altered so that this loggia now looks out on to a delightful enclosed garden with a small lawn and beds of flowers leading to a stream. The drive is on the opposite side and enters beneath an arch joining the twin brick lodges that guard the forecourt with its simple circular drive and panels of well mown turf. Elsewhere the outlines of the original rectangular design are still to be observed and the formation of beds and borders follows in the main a similar geometric plan relieved by generous planting of herbaceous perennials, shrubs and roses.

**67. CRANBORNE: THE LAWN AND BORDERS ON THE FAR SIDE OF THE HOUSE**

**68. CREECH GRANGE: FORMAL BEDS WITH THE CANAL POOL BEYOND**

**Creech Grange, Wareham, Dorset.** This lovely Tudor Manor House is placed in a deep fold of the Purbeck Hills where the natural limestone gives way to stiff clay over which has been deposited a thick layer of leaf mould. The site was heavily planted with broad-leaved and coniferous trees in the nineteenth century and into this setting have been introduced many of the fine rhododendrons which have been so typical of twentieth century woodland planting.

The garden, however, has retained other and more distinctive features in character with the house. Separating house from wood is a fine stretch of artificial water, long and narrow like a canal but without any other formal features and entirely devoid of plants. Between it and the house is a series of formal beds planted with azaleas flanked by hardy palms

and with a fountain playing into a basin in the middle. The contrast between these brilliantly coloured beds and the dark canal beyond is dramatic and is heightened by the surrounding trees which tend to keep the water in shadow.

To the south of the house, separating it from the hill which dominates it, is a large lawn relieved only by a few specimen trees and double lines of fine clipped yews on either side. This lawn serves as a main display ground for the scores of peacocks which are a feature of Creech Grange.

Beyond this smooth rectangle of lawn the well wooded hills rise steeply and provide a dramatic back-drop to the whole scene which is all the more effective because of its simplicity. No plant disturbs the beauty of the house from which even the grass is kept back by a flagged paving.

**69. DARTINGTON HALL: THE GREAT FLIGHT OF STEPS PASSING THROUGH THE HEATHER
GARDEN TO THE HILL WHICH OVERLOOKS THE OPEN-AIR THEATRE**

## 70. DARTINGTON HALL: THE OPEN-AIR STAGE AND TWELVE APOSTLES

**Dartington Hall, Totnes, Devon.** The garden around this fine old mansion, some of which dates from the fourteenth century, has been almost entirely re-designed in the present century by Mr and Mrs Elmhirst who founded the Dartington Trust and began to develop the property as a centre for cultural activities of many kinds including drama, music, ballet and numerous handicrafts. A central feature is a large open-air theatre with grass auditorium and stage. This is flanked on one side by a row of twelve Irish yews, known as the Twelve Apostles, and on the other by a series of grass terraces. Rising ground on three sides of this central open space has been informally planted with trees and shrubs, both as specimens and in groups, and a notable feature is a very wide flight of stone steps running up the hillside opposite the house through a large heather garden. Trees and shrubs have been well sited to provide a series of fine vistas over the surrounding country and across the undulating ground to Dartington Hall itself. A figure of a reclining woman by Henry Moore has been successfully incorporated in this informal setting as a focal point on the hillside. Within the forecourt of the hall a more formal design has been followed but still the planting is almost exclusively of flowering trees and shrubs.

## 71. DARTINGTON HALL: A TYPICAL GRASS WALK IN THE WOODLAND GARDEN

**72. DUNSBOROUGH PARK: THE ROCK
AND WATER GARDEN**

**Dunsborough Park, Ripley, Surrey.** The west
side of the house has been kept open so that there
is a completely unobstructed view of the park beyond.
The only features here are a simple, flagged terrace with some beds for flowers in season and a huge
specimen of the swamp cypress, *Taxodium distichum*.
The main garden is to the north of this open space
and has been designed around the vegetable garden
so that it both conceals and makes use of this necessary but utilitarian feature. First there is a double
herbaceous border parallel with the house and extend-
ing the line of the terrace and then, at an angle to this,
is another long walk backed on one side by the high
wall of the kitchen garden and on the other by a wall-
like hedge of yew. This forms a gaily planted alley
which, if extended, would be centred on the terrace
and is visible from it. The yew hedge also serves to
enclose a formal rose garden, beyond which the scene
completely changes to an extensive rock and water
garden in the natural style which continues right down
to the stream flowing through the estate. To the south
of the house is a small formal garden with dripping
fountain fed by a narrow canal which serves as an
overflow for a swimming pool concealed behind a
mound topped by a summer house.

**73. DUNSBOROUGH PARK: THE DOUBLE
HERBACEOUS BORDER**

**74. EAST LAMBROOK MANOR: COTTAGE
GARDEN TREATMENT OF THE LOW
TERRACES**

**East Lambrook Manor, South Petherton,
Somerset.** Though genuinely a manor house this is
quite a small property and one so snugly ensconced in
the village that it has more the character of an old-
fashioned country cottage. The garden is entirely in
keeping with the house, completely lacking in formality and pretension but packed with good plants
arranged with a deceptive air of carelessness which
conceals a great deal of painstaking design. This is an
intimate garden in which plants are to be studied for
their own worth. Much of it is made on slightly rising
ground which has been terraced with roughly hewn
stone and provided with stone paths and steps for easy
access but is otherwise completely filled with a medley
of plants in the cottage style. A little distance from the
house is a large and well-preserved barn as picturesque
as the house itself. This has been well covered with
climbing plants and the shady strip behind has been
converted into a moist peat garden in which many
rarities thrive. Plants of architectural quality, such as
angelica and *Euphorbia Wulfenii*, are used with fine
effect to add point and emphasis to what might otherwise be a slightly confused picture.

**75. EAST LAMBROOK MANOR: ROCK BED
AND LAWN SEPARATED BY THE DRIVE**

**76. EMMANUEL COLLEGE: FINE TREES
ARE A FEATURE OF THIS GARDEN**

**Emmanuel College, Cambridge.** The garden at
Emmanuel is famous for its trees and for its swans.
The trees include a large liriodendron (tulip tree) and,
in the Fellows' Garden which is partly shut off from
the main garden by a high brick wall, a huge liquidambar which is uncommonly broad in proportion to its
height. There are also fine beeches and one of the first
specimens of *Metasequoia glyptostroboides* to be
planted in England. It has grown very rapidly and is
already making a shapely and graceful tree. As a
setting for all this there are wide lawns and curving
borders of perennials with a few beds for spring and
summer flowers in season. The large oval pool, which
is the home of many water plants as well as of the
swans, is cut out of the lawn in the main garden and
provides a sudden change in texture which is pleasing
though it may be felt that the shape of the pool is
rather too regular for its setting.

The wall which shelters the Fellows' Garden is
almost completely covered by shrubs and climbing
plants including some, such as the pomegranate, which
would be too tender to grow reliably in the open without this protection.

**77. EMMANUEL COLLEGE: THE FAMOUS
LIQUIDAMBAR CAN BE SEEN IN THE
BACKGROUND**

**78. ERIDGE CASTLE: DOUBLE HERBACEOUS BORDERS ENCLOSED BY YEW HEDGES**

**79. ERIDGE CASTLE: THE AVENUE OF TULIP TREES LEADING TO THE HOUSE**

**80. ERIDGE CASTLE: MORE BORDERS OF HERBACEOUS PLANTS**

**Eridge Castle, Sussex.** Eridge is famous for its superb herbaceous borders and for its noble avenue of tulip trees (liriodendron). The latter line the drive that leads to the house and are fine old trees which have now reached their full development. The herbaceous borders are double, separated by a broad grass walk and almost completely enclosed in wall-like hedges of yew which curve inwards at both ends to leave no more than the gap required to accommodate the path. This is an unusual plan but one which proves most effective, giving to the borders a formal frame which suits them well. The borders are of great size and have been exceptionally well planted with bold groups of perennials carefully selected for height, season and colour. They are among the finest examples to be found in the country today of the Edwardian style of herbaceous border into which neither shrubs nor bedding plants obtrude and which, despite their irregular grouping of plants, are as essentially formal in conception as any Victorian bedding scheme. The firm pattern of this garden is emphasised not simply by its encircling hedges but also by the flagstone edges to the borders. Large trees shelter the garden and give it a suitably massive setting without in any way encroaching on it.

**81. ERIDGE CASTLE: A DETAIL OF PLANTING**

**82. EXBURY: ONE OF THE WIDE GRASS RIDES FLANKED BY TREES AND SHRUBS**

**83. EXBURY: A MASSED PLANTING OF DECIDUOUS AZALEAS IN VIVID COLOURS**

**84. EXBURY: RHODODENDRONS AND AZALEAS FLANKING ONE OF THE WOODLAND WALKS**

**Exbury, nr Southampton, Hampshire.** The garden at Exbury is famous for its trees and shrubs and, most of all, for its unsurpassed collection of rhododendrons. It is a garden impossible to write about in terms of design for, in fact, it owes little to the more conventional arts of garden planning. Under the skilful hands of its maker, Mr Lionel de Rothschild, it took shape and grew as his collection of plants increased. It is mainly a woodland garden consisting of large groupings of trees and shrubs separated by wide grass rides which give the long vistas for which Exbury is famous. Because of the great emphasis on rhododendrons it is at its best in spring, but there is, in addition, a sufficient variety of other plants to maintain interest throughout the year, and autumn provides a second peak of colour with berries and turning leaves. Many of the rhododendrons and azaleas are hybrids raised at Exbury and included among them are some of the finest varieties raised in this country. In consequence the garden is of great interest to collectors and connoisseurs of choice plants. Nevertheless it would be a mistake to think of Exbury as simply another collector's garden. Its colour, the beauty of its many fine trees, and the skill with which everything has been disposed to produce a seemingly endless succession of natural pictures make this a garden that every visitor can enjoy however unversed he may be in the names and origins of the plants he is viewing. Water also enters prominently into the scheme in the shape of large lakes which reflect the colours of trees, flowers, and sky. In early spring there are fine displays of naturalised daffodils.

## 85. FIELD PLACE: HERBACEOUS PLANTS GROUPED AROUND THE LAWN

**Field Place, Horsham, Sussex.** Two entirely distinct gardens have been made at Field Place, one surrounding the pleasant old Sussex manor house and the other around a large artificial lake a short distance away. The garden near the house is partially walled and these walls have been used as backgrounds for fine herbaceous borders which have been planned with unusual care, not only to give a succession of flower for several months, but also to present a changing series of colour harmonies. The walls are used to support many climbers such as clematis and roses and there are also beds of bush roses set in the lawn which provides the necessary contrast to all these flowers. The second garden is planted mainly with trees and shrubs, with some herbaceous plants interspersed to give greater colour in summer, and with primulas, spiraeas and other moisture-loving plants in the damp ground around the lake. Though the general treatment here, as in the garden around the house, is natural in the sense in which that term was used by the early twentieth-century reformers of garden design, it never lacks that ordered though apparently artless planning which was an essential part of their principles. Further planting has been carried out in the vegetable garden, notably a magnificent double border of regal lilies.

## 86. FIELD PLACE: A BORDER PLANTED FOR SUCCESSIONAL COLOUR EFFECT

**87. FIELD PLACE: NATURAL PLANTING OF PRIMULAS AND OTHER MOISTURE LOVING PLANTS AT THE LAKESIDE**

**88. FULBROOK HOUSE: DAHLIAS AND OTHER AUTUMN FLOWERS WITH GOLDEN IRISH YEWS**

**Fulbrook House, Godalming, Surrey.** The house is an early example of the work of Sir Edwin Lutyens and it is extremely well placed on rising ground from which fine views can be obtained of the surrounding country. The garden may be considered in two distinct sections, firstly a series of formal terraces rising from the house and providing an appropriate setting for it, and secondly, further afield and out of sight of the house, a woodland garden which is completely informal. On the terraces spring and summer bedding is carried out to maintain as continuous a display as possible. The terraces are further suitably furnished with permanent features such as golden yews, which give them interest at all seasons. In the woodland garden azaleas and acers figure prominently and autumn colour has been given special attention. Fulbrook House provides yet another example of that happy blending of the formal and informal which appears to have been the special genius of the early twentieth century gardeners. It is a garden which admirably performs its purpose of providing a fitting setting for a gracious but not over-elaborate house and at the same time linking it with the Surrey landscape. In conception it is entirely English and, though very different in detail, may be compared with the garden at Abbotswood.

**89. FURZEY: THE HEATHER GARDEN AS SEEN FROM NEAR THE HOUSE**

**Furzey, Minstead, Hampshire.** This is one of the two famous gardens made by the brothers Dalrymple in the first quarter of this century. Furzey was the property of Hugh Dalrymple; Bertram Dalrymple gardened a few miles away at the House-in-the-Wood, Bartley. Despite this close association and the fact that both gardens would come under the general heading 'natural', there is a remarkable difference between them. Whereas the House-in-the-Wood is, as its name implies, surrounded by large trees, Furzey stands on open ground with extensive views across the New Forest. In contrast to the woodland plantings of shade-loving shrubs and plants used by Bertram Dalrymple, his brother at Furzey created a splendid heathland garden in which the open nature of the site has been fully preserved and groupings of shrubs and trees have been used with great skill to break up but not to obscure the view. The house is in keeping with this treatment—a long, low building with thatched roof in the cottage tradition. Heathers are used freely as are many other plants which thrive in acid soils and some of these, such as the New Zealand leptospermums, have found the conditions so much to their liking that they constantly renew themselves from seed.

91. FURZEY: SPRING BEDDING ON THE HOUSE TERRACE

90. FURZEY: DAFFODILS NATURALISED IN THE GRASS

93. THE GARDEN HOUSE: THE VIEW FROM THE VALLEY

92. THE GARDEN HOUSE: ONE OF THE TERRACES

**94. THE GARDEN HOUSE: LONG BORDERS AT THE FOOT OF THE HILL**

**The Garden House, Buckland Monachorum, Devon.** Approaching the Garden House from the road one has no hint of what lies beyond. There is a well kept lawn and a pleasant house, but no more. It is, in consequence, with the added thrill of astonishment that one emerges on the other side to find a garden that is ablaze with flowers from spring to autumn. The ground falls away very steeply and is terraced in such a way that from near the house it is possible to obtain a birds-eye view of almost the whole garden.

The design is straightforwardly suited to the site; a series of more or less rectangular terraces with wide flower borders and either broad grass paths or lawn to separate them. It is, in fact, in the flowers themselves rather than in any novelty of plan that the interest of this garden lies. Most of

these plants are hardy herbaceous perennials with a backbone of good shrubs and climbers. There are many uncommon plants as well as the more familiar kinds and the selection has been made to cover the widest possible season. Full advantage has been taken of the mild South Devon climate, to include many plants that are on the borderline of hardiness and this gives the garden an added interest to the connoisseur of rare plants.

The visitor with less botanical knowledge will be delighted by the freedom of the planting and the great variety of plants that are grown. At the foot of the hill a small, half ruined tower adds a touch of romance to the scene. On one side a high brick wall flanks the garden and gives it increased protection.

**95. GLAN-Y-MAWDDACH: THE VIEW FROM THE HILLSIDE UP THE MAWDDACH ESTUARY**

**Glan-y-Mawddach, Barmouth, Merionethshire.** Few gardens in the British Isles have so fine a natural setting as Glan-y-Mawddach on the steep slopes on the north shore of the great Mawddach estuary which extends from Dolgelly to Barmouth. It commands magnificent views up and down this estuary and across it to the massive bulk of Cader Idris a few miles to the south. Moreover as the estuary is tidal it is a scene which is constantly changing with the ebb and flow of the water.

In such an idyllic place a garden might seem almost an irrelevance, but in fact it has been made with such skill that it fits perfectly into the picture as well as providing many admirable vantage points from which to enjoy it. The garden dates back to Victorian times and contains many of the trees and shrubs that were popular then; wellingtonias and monkey puzzles, blue spruces, Lawson cypresses, tulip trees and rhododendrons. In the shelter provided by these many of the popular shrubs of our own times are established, interplanted with lilies and, in the damper places, primulas.

Near the house there are more formal features, preserved or adapted from the Victorian design, including a small enclosed garden with lily pool. At the highest point of the garden a large rock garden has been fashioned mainly by baring the natural stone of the site. Steep winding paths and steps give access to the various parts of this hillside garden and conveniently placed look-outs provide resting places as well as viewpoints.

96. GLAN-Y-MAWD-
DACH: STEPS LEAD-
ING UP THE HILL-
SIDE AND FLANKED
BY HYDRANGEAS

97. GLAN-Y-MAWD-
DACH: ANOTHER
VIEW OF THE
STEEP SLOPES
HEAVILY PLANTED
WITH TREES,
SHRUBS AND
HERBACEOUS
PLANTS

98. GLAN-Y-MAWD-
DACH: PART OF
THE ROCK GARDEN

**99. THE GRANGE, BENENDEN: JAPANESE CHERRIES UNDERPLANTED WITH FLOWERING SHRUBS**

**The Grange, Benenden, Kent.** Captain Collingwood Ingram, who made this garden, is a recognised authority on flowering cherries and in it he has made a unique collection of these beautiful trees. The design of the garden is informal, wide grass paths leading between the cherries and other trees and shrubs which form the basis of the planting. Captain Collingwood Ingram, like so many twentieth century collectors, is more interested in plants than in garden design but has nevertheless been entirely successful in developing a plan well suited to his purpose of displaying his rare plants to best advantage. He has, in effect, produced a woodland glade in which most of the trees are exotic.

Making use of the shelter provided by the taller shrubs and trees he has established many herbaceous and bulbous rooted plants that maintain interest long after the last of the cherries has flowered, and in autumn The Grange at Benenden has the further attraction of the colour of ripening fruits and foliage. For early spring display there are daffodils plentifully naturalised in the grass and a little later deciduous azaleas are in bloom.

The interest of the garden is undoubtedly increased by the fact that so many of the plants in it have either been raised by Captain Collingwood Ingram or have been brought back by him from his frequent travels in other countries.

## 100. GRAYSWOOD HILL: INFORMAL PLANTATIONS OF TREES AND FLOWERING SHRUBS

**Grayswood Hill, Haslemere, Surrey.** The garden at Grayswood Hill is very much that of a connoisseur of fine plants and it is as a collection rather than as a design that it must be considered. Nevertheless, it is a collection that has been made with excellent taste the individual items of which have been placed so that they enhance the magnificent views towards Black Down Ridge. Moreover it is a fairly old collection, having been started in the last quarter of the nineteenth century, so that the fine trees and shrubs of which it is mainly composed have had ample time to reach their full proportions and display their mature beauty. In treatment the garden is simple, two level terraces of turf and flower borders leading direct to the steep south slopes beyond, which are intersected by paths that wind between wide beds and borders filled with a great variety of exotic trees and shrubs. Autumn colour of leaf and fruit as well as the earlier colour of blossom has been provided for and so this garden has an exceptionally long season of interest. The situation is one of great natural beauty and one of the merits of the garden is that it is admirably suited to the landscape.

## 101. GRAYSWOOD HILL: THE SIMPLE TREATMENT AROUND THE HOUSE

**102. GREAT DIXTER: ELABORATE TOPIARY SPECIMENS ON THE LAWN**

**Great Dixter, Northiam, Sussex.** The original house dates back to the fifteenth century and is a beautiful half timbered building which was enlarged by the addition of a similar fourteenth century manor brought from another part of the country. It is flanked by three oast houses which add their peculiar grace to the rural scene and set the stage for a garden which is obviously romantic in conception. There are many clipped yews and trim hedges which are pleasantly varied in shape. There is a sunken garden, but here again formality has been kept well in hand and the planting is refreshingly varied. Walls are generously covered with good climbing plants and the crevices between paving stones provide a foothold for many alpines. Orchard fruit trees are permitted to approach close to the house on two sides and add to the feeling of a happy compromise between nature and artifice. Bulbs are naturalised beneath the trees and fritillarias are included among them. A long border is filled with shrubs, hardy herbaceous plants and dahlias and it is noticeable that dahlias also figure prominently elsewhere in this garden, prolonging its display into the autumn. Fuchsias and penstemons help to the same end and enhance the old-world effect.

**103. GREAT DIXTER: HERBACEOUS PLANTS AND CLIMBERS SHELTERED BY OAST HOUSES**

**104. HADDON HALL: THE UPPER
TERRACES**

**Haddon Hall, Bakewell, Derby-
shire.** So remarkable is the mediaeval
magnificence of Haddon Hall that it is
only natural and fitting that the garden
should play a subsidiary part. Rectangular terraces are cut into the steep slopes
to the south of the building towards the
River Wye. The walls retaining these terraces are necessarily very deep and they
have been built dry of local stone with a
very marked batter. In consequence they
have provided an ideal home for a variety
of rock plants which cover the stone
work with large drifts of foliage and
flowers. A great flight of dry stone steps
leads from the river past these terraces
straight to the chapel whence a narrow
terrace leads to the upper garden which
spreads a cool green carpet of lawn in
front of the house broken only by a few
simple flower beds.

**105. HADDON HALL: ONE OF THE
MANY HEAVILY BUTTRESSED
STONE WALLS**

**106. HASCOMBE COURT: THE ROCK GARDEN**

**Hascombe Court, nr Godalming, Surrey.** This garden is famous for its herbaceous borders which are of unusual size and have been sited with considerable skill. Twin borders separated by exceptionally wide grass walks are centred on the house on both sides. To the east they are terminated by a substantially constructed stone summer house, but to the west the land falls away conveniently so that it has been possible to open a vista to the distant fields and woods. All these borders are very wide as well as being unusually long and they have been planted with great boldness.

The land falls away even more steeply to the south and here a great rock garden has been made on the hillside terminating at the foot in a water garden. The planting of the rock garden is unusually bold, and shrubs are used freely.

**107. HASCOMBE COURT: A SECTION OF THE DOUBLE HERBACEOUS BORDERS**

**108. HATFIELD HOUSE: THE OLD PALACE FROM THE GARDEN OF HATFIELD HOUSE**

**Hatfield House, Hatfield, Hertfordshire.** Hatfield House was built early in the seventeenth century, on land which had previously formed part of the estate of Hatfield Old Palace. The new house was made on a long, but rather narrow plateau of land above and to the south of the old building and as some of the latter has been preserved to the present day there are, in fact, two houses and two gardens though so closely are the latter related both physically and in design that they may be considered as one. Much of the basic design has been preserved from the time the property was created by the first Earl of Salisbury. In front of the old palace is a more or less square parterre occupied by beds in the form of concentric circles. Around Hatfield House itself there are wide areas of lawns broken by more elaborately patterned beds. The fine tracery of the stone balustrades to the terraces, and the magnificent staircases which sweep down from them, add to the grandeur of this deliberately architectural garden.

**109. HATFIELD HOUSE: ELABORATE BEDDING ON THE TERRACES**

**110. HENLEY HALL: THE LILY POOL TO THE EAST OF THE LIME AVENUE**

**Henley Hall, Ludlow, Shropshire.** This fine old house which bears evidence of Jacobean work as well as later extensive alterations in the Queen Anne and Georgian manner, is approached through an avenue of limes and it is on either side of this avenue that much of the garden has been created in the present century. To the east of this avenue is a large formal lily pool surrounded by a lawn which is itself enclosed, partly by low terraces retained by dry walls and partly by trees and shrubs. It is a garden in which formal and informal elements have been very pleasantly welded and it is conceived on suitably spacious lines. To the west of the lime avenue is a rock and water garden with spring bulbs naturalised in thin woodland. Beyond the house the Long Garden leads to the deer park. Double herbaceous borders flank this garden and remind us again how much the whole design has been inspired by the writings and practice of Gertrude Jekyll and William Robinson.

**111. HENLEY HALL: TERRACING EMPHASISED BY SKILFUL PLANTING**

**112. HEVER CASTLE: THE MOAT AND HERBACEOUS PLANTS AROUND THE CASTLE**

**Hever Castle, Edenbridge, Kent.** The castle is a small one dating back to the thirteenth century, though much of it was reconstructed in Tudor times. It is a building of very romantic appearance with high battlemented walls completely surrounded by a broad moat. It was acquired early in the present century by the first Lord Astor who proceeded to make what are virtually three distinct gardens. The first, which surrounds the castle, is typically English in style. The moat itself is planted with water lilies and the narrow strip of ground between moat and castle is filled with herbaceous plants. A broad drive, leading through an orchard to the castle entrance, is flanked by topiary specimens in yew and the orchard itself is filled with daffodils. On the other side of the castle is a small maze and a series of little formal gardens hedged in yew one of which contains a set of giant chessmen also cut in yew. Nothing could be more in keeping with the scene.

A short way off one enters a series of large formal gardens of totally different character. Conceived in the Italian style they contain large quantities of statuary and stone ornaments and numerous architectural features. At one point there is a most elaborate grotto filled with ferns and other shade-loving plants which is said to be a copy of the Gallery of a Hundred Fountains in the Villa d'Este at Tivoli. All this terminates in a vast lake dug by hand and bordered by an elaborate colonnaded piazza on which stands a notably beautiful fountain guarded by female figures.

Though these Italian gardens are not at all in character either with the castle or with the garden which surrounds it, they are so far from them and are so well screened by walls and trees that they form a unit on their own entirely separate from the rest. With the exception of the alterations at Blenheim Palace it is probable that nothing quite so elaborate or architectural has been attempted by any other twentieth-century gardener.

The third garden is in the woodland style, natural in conception and containing many fine trees and shrubs. A large winter garden which was once a feature of Hever has been demolished and the site converted into a rose garden from which a rock garden leads directly into this woodland.

**113. HEVER CASTLE: A SECTION OF THE ITALIAN GARDEN IN WHICH ORNAMENTS ARE FREELY USED AMONG THE FLOWERS**

114. HEVER
CASTLE: FORMAL
GARDENS
HEDGED IN YEW
AND WITH GIANT
CHESSMEN ALSO
CUT IN YEW

115. HEVER
CASTLE:
COLONNADED
PIAZZA AT THE
SIDE OF THE
GREAT LAKE

## 116. HIDCOTE: THE GREAT ALLEY LEADING TO THE TERRACE

**Hidcote, Chipping Campden, Gloucestershire.**
The interest of this famous garden resides partly in
its fine collection of plants, but even more in its unusual and effective design. The site, on top of the
Cotswolds, is naturally exposed, and the designer's
problem has been to combine a due amount of enclosure, to give protection from the wind, with the feeling
of space without which no really great garden can be
created. This problem has been solved by giving the
garden two very long but comparatively narrow vistas
at right angles to one another and then, around these
main axes, creating a series of intimate gardens each
different in character though allied in style. The more
important of the two vistas is the Great Alley which,
starting near the house, continues through flower
borders backed by yew hedges and eventually passes
up a flight of stone steps and through wrought iron
gates to a terrace in which standard hornbeams have
been trimmed to produce a massive rampart of foliage.
The second axis is a broad grass avenue bordered by
clipped beech and terminated at its farthest point by
massive wrought iron gates. The severity of this avenue
is in marked contrast to the lavish planting of the
Great Alley. The intimate gardens include one almost
completely occupied by a huge circular basin of water.

## 117. HIDCOTE: THE TERRACE ON WHICH STANDARD HORNBEAMS GIVE MASSIVE ENCLOSURE

118. HIDCOTE: THE GREAT ALLEY LOOKING TOWARDS THE HOUSE FROM THE END OF THE HORNBEAM TERRACE

119. HIDCOTE: ONE OF THE INTIMATE GARDENS NEARLY FILLED BY A HUGE CIRCULAR BASIN OF WATER

**120. HIGHDOWN: THE POOL AND ROCK GARDEN WHICH FLANK THE CHALK PIT**

**Highdown, Goring-on-Sea, Sussex.** A couple of miles inland from Goring-by-Sea a hill rises gently from the flat coastal belt—an outrider of the South Downs which lie farther back. The hill is surmounted by a large chalk quarry and it is in front of this that Sir Frederick Stern chose to build his house. He then proceeded to make his garden, in part on the sloping ground in front of the house, and in part in the quarry itself, a feat which some experts pronounced to be im-

possible. The result is a garden of great interest as well as of uncommon beauty. The vertical back of the quarry has been converted into a mosaic of leaf colour, partly by covering it with ivies and other climbing plants and partly by placing fine conifers in the rubble slope at its foot. This slope has itself been converted into a great rock garden in which a surprising variety of plants thrive, and the flatter ground in the centre of the quarry has been grassed and provided with a pool for

**121. HIGHDOWN: DAFFODILS NATURALISED IN THE OLD CHALK PIT**

water lilies and other aquatics, with another rock garden leading away from it.

Most of the remaining garden has been designed on fairly
simple lines with large borders filled with a miscellany of
herbaceous plants, bulbs and shrubs and divided by wide
grass paths. Sir Frederick Stern is a keen collector of plants
with a special interest in irises, daffodils, peonies, lilies,
eremuri and roses, all of which figure prominently in his
garden. Because of this wide range of plants interest is
maintained for an unusually long period; indeed it would be
true to say that this is a garden that is never without flowers.
Proximity to the sea and excellent air drainage make it possible to grow some slightly tender plants.

From the house and the terrace in front of it there are fine
views of coast and sea. The drive drops steeply away from the
house and daffodils are naturalised in the grass beside it.

**122. HIGHGATE HILL: THE HILLSIDE AS SEEN THROUGH THE STONE COLONNADED PERGOLA**

**No. 41 Highgate West Hill, London.** So skilfully has the landscape gardener worked at Lady Crosfield's famous garden on Highgate West Hill that it is difficult to realize it is situated alongside a busy London thoroughfare within a few miles of Charing Cross. The house stands close to the road, and together with a walled garden on three levels which falls away from it, provides a complete barrier between the world outside and the lovely parkland that lies beyond. The terrace gardens are formal in treatment and terminate in a small rose garden separated by a low wall and stone-colonnaded pergola from the park. It is from this point that one of the loveliest views is to be obtained, down the well-timbered slopes that are heavily planted with daffodils, over the valley to Primrose Hill in the distance.

**123. THE HOUSE IN THE WOOD: NATURALISED DAFFODILS AND CORNUS NUTTALLII**

**The House in the Wood, Bartley, Hampshire.** This is in some ways the more famous of the two notable gardens made by the Dalrymple brothers. While Bertram worked on his open heathland site at Minstead, Hugh was making an attractive natural woodland garden at Bartley in which rhododendrons and primulas play major roles. Of design there is little for all that was necessary was to give access to the various parts of the garden by cutting walks through the trees. Beside these walks and in larger clearings, ornamental trees and shrubs have been established. In the moister places great drifts of *Primula pulverulenta* have become naturalised, and it was in this garden that the many pink forms of this primula, known as the Bartley strain, were produced. At one end of the garden is a glade entirely filled with deciduous azaleas.

**124. THE HOUSE IN THE WOOD: THE DRIVE WITH VIBURNUM FRAGRANS IN THE FOREGROUND**

**125. THE HOUSE IN THE WOOD: THE BARTLEY STRAIN OF PRIMULA PULVÉRULENTA**

**126. HUNGERDOWN: THE LONG TERRACE AND
BORDERS OF SHRUBS, ROSES AND
HERBACEOUS PLANTS**

**Hungerdown, Seagry, Chippenham, Wiltshire.** This
is a garden laid out by a professional landscape architect,
Mr Percy Cane, but modified by an owner who loves plants
and knows what he likes. Thus the many old world roses
which grow so well at Hungerdown are no part of Mr Cane's
original plan though they fit in very well with it. The house
is situated on gently rising land above the Avon in its upper
reaches and has been provided with a very solid and satisfactory setting by the creation of a series of large terraces on
two sides. These have been variously planned and planted.
One is long and flanked on either side by mixed borders of
herbaceous plants, shrubs and roses and with a fine vista
through the rest of the garden. Another smaller terrace is
square and flagged with central pool and fountain and a
third is a simple grass plot with flower borders on three
sides. Beyond this terraced area the land falls and then rises
again, giving the designer a wonderful opportunity to create
long vistas between irregular groups of trees and shrubs
separated by wide grass walks. This is a fine example of
twentieth century informal and labour-saving planning.

**127. HUNGERDOWN: THE CENTRAL VISTA
THROUGH THE INFORMAL TREE AND SHRUB
GARDENS**

**128. JULIANS: THE HOUSE AND ENCLOSED FORECOURT SEEN FROM THE DRIVE**

**129. JULIANS: THE WALK THROUGH THF OLD WALLED GARDEN SEEN FROM THE WATER LILY POOL**

**130. JULIANS: HERBACEOUS BORDERS FLANKING THE CENTRAL WALK IN THE OLD WALLED VEGETABLE GARDEN**

**Julians, Buntingford, Hertfordshire.** The house is Georgian in appearance though much of it was not actually built until 1937. It is, nevertheless, a pleasant and dignified house particularly on the south front and, very properly, much of the planting on this side has been kept discreetly away from the house so that it in no way detracts from its beauty. An open forecourt is flanked by brick walls generously covered with climbing roses, but otherwise there is little in the way of beds close to the house. Farther away the land falls a little and has been terraced, and on this lower level there is a long herbaceous border and a rose hedge formed mainly of hybrid musk varieties. Climbing roses cover the walls of the large ballroom and behind the house roses are again used freely in a rectangular walled garden on two levels. Here a notable feature on the lower terrace is a circular lily pool with a fine bronze statue of a seal. The planting around this lower terrace is mainly with red and yellow roses but on the upper terrace old-fashioned varieties predominate in the lovely shades of pink, claret and soft purple that were popular in Victorian times. Beyond this garden, but concealed from it by a brick wall, is a large swimming pool also surrounded by roses.

One wall of the water-lily terrace was originally the boundary of a large walled vegetable garden. The whole of this has been devoted to shrubs and herbaceous plants in a series of rectangular borders which are more complex in design than is at first apparent. Though the first impression is of twin borders separated by a wide grass path, closer inspection reveals that there are, in fact, a number of separate borders with narrow paths between them. This part of the garden is of great interest not only because of the skilful way in which shrubs and herbaceous plants are associated, but also for the unusual design which has the effect of revealing its elements little by little and always with an element of surprise. The main grass walk is centred on the seal statue.

**131. KETTERINGHAM HALL: CLIPPED IRISH YEWS FLANKING THE LONG WALK**

**Ketteringham Hall, Norwich, Norfolk.** The house is Tudor and well preserved and the garden, most of which must have been made in the late nineteenth or early twentieth centuries, is perfectly in keeping both with its dignity and elaboration. In front there is simply a wide drive separating the house from well-kept playing fields (the house is now used as a preparatory school). At the back there are formal beds, some filled with bedding plants or annuals in season, some with roses, and this section leads to a long walk flanked on one side by specimen Irish yews of considerable size and on the other by a high wall of old brick. On the third and long side of the building facing a stretch of artificial water which has the appearance of a river, the ground has been terraced, the upper level being formally planned and retained by a brick wall topped by pinnacles in character with the building and the lower level being a wide sweep of grass leading to the water's edge, broken only by a few specimen trees. As in so many old gardens room has been found in the kitchen garden for flower borders as well as vegetables. The garden is greatly enhanced by the many fine trees that surround it at a sufficient distance to give enclosure without confinement. It is not a garden of any particular date or style but rather one that has grown through the years and in the making of which many hands have played a part.

**132. KIFTSGATE: A BORDER IN WHICH FOLIAGE PLANTS FIGURE PROMINENTLY**

**Kiftsgate, Chipping Campden, Gloucestershire.**
This beautiful garden is situated very near to Hidcote high up on the Cotswolds, but unlike Hidcote it is on the lip of the hill with magnificent views towards Malvern across the Vale of Evesham. The house, though originally a typical Cotswold manor, has been altered considerably by the addition of a colonnaded portico and terrace which give it a rather formal and dignified appearance. This has provided a setting for a garden in which roses and flowering shrubs figure prominently but with a difference. The roses are encouraged to grow into very large bushes and many old fashioned varieties and species are included. The shrubs are freely mixed with these roses and herbaceous plants are also brought into the scheme, but always with definite colour schemes in mind. These colours are very largely those rich or subdued shades of crimson and purple, old rose, soft pink and mauve that one tends to associate with tapestry and, indeed, this interesting garden has many of the elements of a fine tapestry design. Because of its great reliance on roses it is at its best in June and July but it is by no means a one season garden. The steep hillside has also been well planted and, at a lower level, is a semi-circular garden in which lilies are added as a further element in the design. Some of the best views of the surrounding country are to be obtained from this lower level.

**133. KIFTSGATE: THE ROSE GARDEN NEAR THE HOUSE**

**134. KIFTSGATE: THE HILLSIDE LEADING TO THE LOWER GARDEN**

**135. KIFTSGATE: A BORDER OF SHRUBS, OLD-FASHIONED ROSES AND HERBACEOUS PLANTS**

**136. KINGSTON RUSSELL HOUSE: THE GREAT RECTANGLES OF TOPIARY UNRELIEVED BY FLOWERS OR OTHER PLANTS**

**Kingston Russell House, Dorchester, Dorset.** A modern topiary garden is somewhat of a novelty but that is precisely what has been made at Kingston Russell House. The house itself has two distinct faces, a classical Palladian front to the west facing the road, and a King Charles II elevation on the east and garden side. It is as a fitting setting to this rather severely rectangular face that the topiary garden has been made. Here are no fantastic shapes of birds or chessmen, but straight cut hedges with, for ornamentation, no more than an occasional arch or miniature tower. The hedges enclose rectangles of turf and are themselves regularly arranged along both sides of a wide grass walk centred at one end of the house, and at the other by a columned hemicycle which matches the classic lines of the building. Midway is a fountain pool to the south of which, off the main axis of the garden, are larger enclosures with higher yew hedges and containing simple flower beds. This design was conceived and carried out by Mr George Gribble soon after he purchased the property in 1913. The rectangles of yew match those of the house in form but contrast startlingly with the light coloured stonework. Both house and garden also provide a somewhat dramatic contrast to the softly contoured countryside. Flowers inevitably play a very minor role in this highly architectural garden.

**137. LEONARDSLEE: THE HOUSE SEEN ACROSS THE VALLEY; THE MAIN WOODLAND PLANTING IS TO THE RIGHT**

**138. LEONARDSLEE: AZALEAS IN THE WOODLAND**

**Leonardslee, Lower Beeding, Sussex.** The hundred acres of this magnificent garden are in the main woodland situated on two sides of a steep valley in which there are several 'hammer' ponds fed by a stream. The site has such great natural beauty that little in the nature of formal planning was either necessary or desirable. Apart from a lawn near the house, broken by shrub borders and commanding a fine view across the valley, and also a large rock garden also near the house, all the planting at Leonardslee has been carried out in the natural woodland and around the stream and 'hammer' ponds in the valley. Winding paths lead down the steep slopes and permit a variety of views of the scenery and planting, but otherwise play no very significant part in the design. The delight of Leonardslee lies in its blaze of colour in spring when azaleas and rhododendrons are at their best. The garden was made by Sir Edmund Loder, who was himself a keen rhododendron breeder, and one of the most famous of hybrid rhododendrons, *R. Loderi*, was raised there. Many huge bushes of this large-flowered and very fragrant variety are to be seen in the gardens, some of these dating from the original plantings about 1903. Magnolias and camellias also grow very freely at Leonardslee and add to the glory of the spring display.

**139. LEONARDSLEE: ONE OF THE 'HAMMER' PONDS**

**140. LEVENS HALL: SOME OF THE ELABORATE TOPIARY SPECIMENS**

**Levens Hall, Kendal, Westmorland.** The glory of this garden is in its topiary. There are few gardens in the country where so many and varied specimens of this art are to be found and fewer still where they are so well preserved. The house dates back to the early seventeenth century and the garden is also very old in conception. The topiary specimens, formed in yew and box, flank the house on the east side and are themselves displayed on an elaborate parterre of formal beds in which, no doubt, equally elaborate bedding schemes were once carried out. Today a simpler form of planting must be adopted to meet the changed conditions of labour but there is still splendid colour in these beds to contrast with the sombre green of box and yew. The shapes and sizes of the clipped shrubs are oddly assorted and they are not placed in any regular plan though they are planted in large rectangular beds separated by wide gravelled paths. The effect is that of some colossal chess board entirely conceived in living material and with the game in play.

**141. THE LODGE: THE ELABORATELY DESIGNED WALLED GARDEN WITH ITS CANAL POOL**

**The Lodge, Sandy, Bedfordshire.** Unlike so many twentieth-century gardens, formal features are prominent in this garden. The main garden is terraced and has a large stone pool of fairly elaborate design into which fountains play, and around which are formal beds filled with spring and summer flowers in season. There is a solidly built, stone colonnaded pergola and other features which turn one's thoughts to the gardens of France and Italy. Even more is this true when one enters the very elaborately designed walled garden which forms a kind of secret or private garden in the continental manner. Elaborately carved stone seats, statues and a formal canal pool complete the impression of good design in which architecture plays the major role and plants are used as an embellishment.

Because of its firm design this is a garden that can be visited with pleasure at any time of the year in contrast to so many of the gardens of its period which are only attractive for a season.

**142. THE LODGE: THE MAIN TERRACE AND COLONNADED PERGOLA**

**143. THE LODGE: THE STONE POOL AND FOUNTAINS ON THE TERRACE**

**144. LUDSTONE HALL: THE KNOT GARDEN
SEEN FROM THE HOUSE**

**Ludstone Hall, Wolverhampton, Shropshire.** It
is fitting that this romantic Jacobean house, completely
surrounded by a moat, should have a knot garden as one
of its main features. This knot garden lies to the east of
the main drive from which it is shut off by a broad and
high hedge, and to the west of the drive, equally concealed from view except from the house front, is another
garden, more modern in conception with wide lawn margined by a serpentine border of herbaceous plants. The
hedges and topiary specimens in the knot garden are of
box, some of the designs being entirely carried out in this
and showing the formalised hearts, spades, clubs and
diamonds of playing cards. Other beds are partly filled
with rose bushes edged by box. There are also topiary
specimens in the form of spirals and balls and a sundial
as a centrepiece.

The old moat has also been brought into the garden
scheme, many water lilies having been successfully established in it. The whole garden has an appearance of enclosure and sophistication pleasantly at variance with the
open park-land which surrounds it.

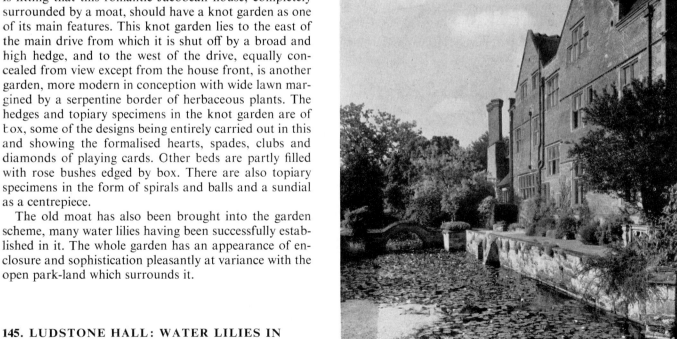

**145. LUDSTONE HALL: WATER LILIES IN
THE MOAT**

**146. LYMPNE HOUSE: THE DARK FORMS OF TOPIARY CONTRASTED WITH STONE ORNAMENTS**

**Lympne House, Lympne, Kent.** The garden is well known for its cherries which here have been used in a much more formal setting than those of Captain Collingwood Ingram at Benenden, not so far away. Well grown hedges enclose the various sections of this garden and an interesting detail is that many of these hedges have been formed of escallonia. Another notable feature is the row of large specimens of *Cupressus macrocarpa* guarding one of the outer walks from which a magnificent view can be obtained across Romney Marsh. Clipped shrubs add further to the ordered appearance of this garden which nevertheless, despite its many formal features, is in the twentieth-century tradition and makes good use of perennial plants whether they be trees, shrubs or of herbaceous character. Because of this balance between architectural and horticultural elements this is a garden to be studied for its design as much as for its planting. Statuary and other stone ornaments are well used, often with the dark background of the hedges to emphasise their form and whiteness.

**147. LYMPNE HOUSE: FLOWERING CHERRIES IN A FORMAL SETTING**

**148. MINTERNE: RHODODENDRONS BESIDE A WOODLAND PATH IN THE VALLEY**

**Minterne, Cerne Abbas, Dorset.** The garden at Minterne is sharply divided into two parts, each of which could well exist entirely independent of the other. Around the house, which is a dignified structure designed by Leonard Stokes in 1903, there is a simple landscape garden in which a large stretch of lawn sweeps nearly to the building itself from which it is separated by a flagged terrace. A ha-ha permits this lawn to merge imperceptibly into the adjoining meadows. Fine trees and a few bold groups of shrubs provide the principal ornament though on a slightly lower level there are also formal rose beds set in the grass.

Passing from this ordered scene through a wicket gate, one immediately starts to descend into the valley on the edge of which Minterne has been built. This has provided Lord Digby with the ideal site in which to make an extensive natural planting of rhododendrons and other shrubs. Scattered about on the open slopes of the valley or sheltered by the fine trees that grow in it, they give the impression of being native to the site rather than of having been planted. A broad stream flows in the valley providing a natural boundary to the garden and giving further opportunity for the naturalisation of moisture-loving plants.

**149. MONTACUTE HOUSE: THE
ENCLOSED GARDEN SEEN
FROM THE HOUSE**

**Montacute House, Yeovil, Somer-
set.** By general consent the garden at
Montacute is one of the most perfect
formal gardens in the British Isles. It
has been said of it that it combines the
nobility of the Renaissance gardens of
Italy with the softness and colour of
England, and this may be considered a
just description. Yet the garden is essentially simple in conception, consisting of
three considerable rectangular areas of
turf the two most important of which are
situated on either side of a wide gravel
path. These areas are similar in size but
differ remarkably in treatment. One,
centred on the house, is entirely enclosed,
on three sides by stone walls surmounted
by delicate balustrading, and on the
fourth by the building itself. Two stone
pavilions of exquisite design stand at
the two further corners of this garden
and two lantern-like ornaments of stone
give further character to the walls.

**150. MONTACUTE HOUSE: THE
SUNKEN GARDEN AND
WATER BASIN**

**151. MUNCASTER CASTLE: THE VALLEY AND VIEW OF THE DISTANT MOUNTAINS**

Borders beneath these walls are generously planted with herbaceous plants, roses and some shrubs.

The second area is sunken and is surrounded by a low stone wall, so that it can be viewed from above. The treatment is much more severe, with dark hedges of yew and specimen Irish yews ranged like sentinels around the lawns. In the centre is a large stone basin of water entirely surrounded by delicate stone balustrading. Flowering plants are confined to one side where there is a wide border of old-fashioned roses and rose species.

This is a garden in which architecture plays a major role and plants are rightly subservient to it, performing the role of emphasising and diversifying the design without in any degree obscuring it. Outside this formal setting is the park, ordered, but natural and providing the fitting contrast to the more sophisticated charms of the garden.

**Muncaster Castle, Eskdale, Cumberland.** This imposing castle stands on a ridge of land near the foot of Eskdale commanding magnificent views up the valley to the mountains around Scafell. It is a position of great natural beauty and, in planting the garden, Sir John Ramsden has had this very much in mind. One of the principal formal features is a great curved terrace of grass, half a mile in length, backed by rhododendrons and other flowering shrubs and bordered by a low hedge of clipped yew and box, across which an unimpeded view of the mountains can be obtained. Below the castle the land drops away sharply to rise again equally steeply on the other side of a narrow valley or ghyll. These further slopes have been generously planted with azaleas and other flowering shrubs which colour the whole hillside in spring. At the head of this valley there are massed plantings of hydrangeas which prolong the floral display into the summer and autumn.

To the west of the castle the treatment is more conventional —a large area of lawn partly surrounded by a belt of shrubs in beds which in earlier times were used for bedding-out plants and still retain some of their formal features. Here, also, are many Japanese azaleas which help to make Muncaster spectacular in autumn as well as in spring.

**152. MUNCASTER CASTLE: THE GREAT CURVED TERRACE OF GRASS**

**153. MUNCASTER CASTLE: THE GARDEN TO THE WEST OF THE CASTLE**

**154. MUNCASTER CASTLE: THE VALLEY AND FAR HILLSIDE ON WHICH AZALEAS HAVE BEEN
MASSED AMONG THE TREES**

**155. NEWBY HALL: DOUBLE HERBACEOUS BORDERS AND GRASS WALK LEADING TO THE RIVER**

**156. NEWBY HALL: THE ROCK AND WATER GARDEN PLANTED ON UNUSUALLY BOLD LINES**

**157. NEWBY HALL: THE FINE VISTA TO THE HOUSE FROM THE RIVER**

**Newby Hall, Skelton, Yorkshire.** The garden around this red brick Queen Anne house represents a happy blending between Victorian design and twentieth century modifications. The principal feature of the garden is the long grass walk centred on the south front of the house and flanked by excellent herbaceous borders. This walk leads directly to the River Ure and the borders are backed by closely trimmed hedges which give added firmness to this main axis of design. To the east there is a large walled garden and to the west rock and water gardens, which owe something to the Japanese style, and good modern shrubberies.

Close to the house the treatment of the garden is simple and is more severely formal. A simple grass terrace on the south front is broken by a large circular lily pool with central group of statuary. To the west the slightly sloping land has been terraced on two levels, the upper terrace being a plain rectangle of grass bordered by a row of Irish yews. Beyond these terraces to the north a vista has been contrived between groups of flowering shrubs.

The whole effect is dignified yet colourful and there is plenty to interest the plantsman as well as the student of garden design. It would be difficult to find a better example of the essentially formal character of herbaceous borders when well planned and planted.

**158. NYMANS: HERBACEOUS PLANTS AND SHRUBS IN A FORMAL SETTING**

**159. NYMANS: AZALEAS AND EXOTIC TREES PLANTED FOR NATURAL EFFECT**

**160. NYMANS: ELABORATE TOPIARY AND HARDY PLANTS IN THE WALLED GARDEN**

**Nymans, Handcross, Sussex.** This is a collector's garden in the sense that it contains a great many rare and interesting plants, but the collection has been made and arranged with such excellent taste that it can be enjoyed as a series of pictures even by those who have no knowledge of plants. In many ways the most distinctive part of this very large garden is the walled garden lying between the top drive and what remains of the house, much of which was destroyed by fire. This walled garden is formal in plan and contains other formal features such as a stone basin and some elaborately shaped topiary specimens. Yet it is mainly planted with the flowering shrubs and herbaceous perennials which are more commonly seen in less formal settings. Elsewhere the garden follows more conventional lines. There are splendid beds of azaleas displayed on the lawn in front of the house, a rock garden, an arboretum, a pinetum, a heather garden and a great assortment of ornamental trees and shrubs, many of which are on the borderline of tenderness but thrive in this southern garden with its excellent air drainage. Nymans is an all-season garden because of its great variety of plants and the firm lines of its design. Nevertheless it is at its loveliest in the spring and early summer.

**161. OCKHAM MILL HOUSE: THE GARDEN SEPARATING THE HOUSE FROM THE MILL STREAM**

**Ockham Mill House, Ripley, Surrey.** It is fitting that this rather romantic old water mill should have a garden in which water plays a very large part. Full use has been made of the natural features of the site to grow a great variety of moisture loving plants such as primulas and astilbes along the banks of small streams which intertwine with informal paths in a setting of good trees and shrubs. Between the house and the main millstream a simpler and more formal design has been adopted, well kept lawns sloping down to the stream and being intersected by a stepping stone path of old mill stones. Shrubs and herbaceous plants provide brilliant colour in season, but it is for its restfulness and its sense of rural charm that Ockham Mill House is mainly remarkable.

**162. PACKWOOD HOUSE: TOPIARY SPECIMENS REPRESENTING THE SERMON ON THE MOUNT**

**Packwood House, Hockley Heath, Warwickshire.**
The most extraordinary feature of this garden is the collection of clipped yews, first made by John Fetherston during the Commonwealth, which is said to represent the Sermon on the Mount. This yew garden is in the form of a large rectangle at a little distance from the house and partly enclosed by a stout hedge. First there are numerous yews in conical form and of varying size which appear to be in procession and are supposed to represent the multitude proceeding to the mount. Beyond these is a transverse walk bordered by twelve larger yews which are known as the Apostles and in the centre are four trees of exceptional size called the Evangelists. Between the Evangelists one great cone of yew reached by a spiral way enclosed in yew hedges is the Master. The

**163. PARK HOUSE: LAWNS SO ENCIRCLED THAT THEY APPEAR LIKE WOODLAND GLADES**

**164. PARK HOUSE: THE OLD STABLE-YARD NOW FILLED WITH PLANTS**

**165. PARK HOUSE: PLANTING IN THE ENGLISH COTTAGE STYLE OUTSIDE THE STUDIO**

fame of the Packwood yews has tended to obscure the fact that the garden has other and more genuinely horticultural features. The approach to the yew garden is through a lovely flower garden, partly enclosed by walls and with fine borders of herbaceous plants and a sunken rose garden beautifully designed and proportioned. Four elegant stone gazebos stand at the corners of this flower garden.

**Park House, Kensington, London.** Here is a garden made in the heart of a great city and completely surrounded by buildings which nevertheless has been so carefully planned and planted that it gives the illusion of a peacefully sequestered country garden. The secret lies in the good use of trees and foliage plants to cut out the ugly features that surround the garden and concentrate attention on those that are beautiful—such as the spire of St Paul's, Onslow Square, which, seen

above a mass of luxuriant growth, might well be the steeple of a village church. The design is simple and in the main follows the familiar English tradition of a pleasantly informal lawn surrounded by flower borders with a lily pool, dry walls well filled with alpines and, of course, plenty of roses. But here the roses are mainly species such as the vigorous cream-flowered *Rosa moschata* which scrambles up into a tree, or the equally free flowering *R. filipes* which covers the stone balustrade of a small terrace to one side of the lawn.

What were once the stables of the house have been converted into a studio which looks much like a country cottage, and near this there is a tumbled mass of simple flowers in the true cottage style. The old stable yard, which separates studio from house, has not escaped the gardener's skill, for it has been brought right into the general scheme with a variety of plants in tubs and pots which can be changed or renewed as season and circumstance warrant.

**166. POWIS CASTLE: THE GREAT TERRACES AND TOPIARY SPECIMENS SEEN FROM THE VALLEY**

**Powis Castle, Welshpool, Montgomeryshire.** The hanging gardens of Powis Castle are famous throughout the world. They were created early in the eighteenth century though it is by no means certain who was responsible for their design. He must have been a very considerable artist to design a setting so appropriate for the rosy-red bastions of this romantic building standing in so prominent a position upon its narrow ridge of rock. The gardens are in steep terraces to the south of the castle. From the front they appear far narrower than their depth though from above this is seen to be an optical illusion. Great buttresses and cones of yews emphasise the height of the terraces and increase their dramatic effect. The central section of the first section rests on a brick loggia with eight arches. It is on this terrace that many of the largest yews are placed. Below the second terrace is a great orangery and along its balustrade are life-size lead figures of shepherds and maidens. From the fourth terrace the ground slopes to the valley below and flowering shrubs are grouped informally. At the foot of the hill a great expanse of level mown grass adds the final touch of emphasis to the whole dramatic scene.

167. POWIS CASTLE: THE VIEW FROM THE BALUSTRADED TERRACE ABOVE THE ORANGERY, LOOKING ACROSS THE VALLEY

**168. PYLEWELL PARK: THE FORMAL
GARDEN SEEN FROM THE HOUSE**

**Pylewell Park, Lymington, Hampshire.**
Though there is a formal flower garden around
the house, the main horticultural interest at Pylewell Park is to be found some distance away
across a stream which bisects the garden. The
stream itself has been well planted in the modern
natural manner and beyond it is a fine example of
woodland planting in which rhododendrons,
azaleas, camellias and other shrubs play the
major role and trees perform the subsidiary part
of providing shelter. The garden extends right to
the banks of the Solent and the treatment becomes
wilder as one approaches the water. This is a good
example of the present-day trend towards labour-
saving planting for large-scale landscape effects.
The garden is also of great interest to plant lovers
because of its many rare or unusual species, some
of which are not regarded as fully hardy in most
parts of the country though here they thrive on
account of their proximity to the sea.

**169. PYLEWELL PARK: THE POOL IN
THE WOODLAND GARDENS**

**170. ROCKINGHAM CASTLE: THE ROSE GARDEN ENCLOSED IN YEW**

**Rockingham Castle, Market Harborough, Northamptonshire.** When a garden surrounds a building so notably picturesque as Rockingham Castle, its duty is to embellish without concealing the architect's work. This has been most satisfactorily accomplished at Rockingham. On the east and north where the architecture is most dramatic, there is no garden at all, the severe walls of the castle rising sheer from close cropped turf. It is to the south and west that the garden has been made and broad terraces command an extensive view over the surrounding countryside. Trim flower beds are cut in the turf and great mounded yews, clipped into shapes reminiscent of water-worn rocks, give enclosure and repeat the rugged outlines of the buildings. One section of the garden, devoted to roses, is entirely enclosed by a large oval yew hedge in which archways have been cut. Fine specimen trees, including some old cedars, complete the dignified effect of this garden.

**171. ROCKINGHAM CASTLE: ONE OF THE TERRACES AROUND THE CASTLE**

**172. ROUS LENCH COURT: A GRASS PATH BETWEEN THE MASSIVE HEDGES OF YEW CHARACTERISTIC OF THIS GARDEN**

**Rous Lench Court, Evesham, Worcestershire.** The garden owes much of its charm to the skill of the pleacher and cutter of yew. It is not a garden of fantastic shapes, but one in which massive hedges have been used to emphasise the natural contours of the land which have here been divided into a series of terraces linked by stone steps and divided by balustraded walls. There are tunnels and arbours of yew, and hedges have been used to form aisles and to enclose vistas in the manner beloved by the great continental practitioners of the art of formal gardening. In such a garden flowers are almost an intrusion, the whole picture being painted in the contrasted greens of grass and yew and the grey stone mottled with the growth of mosses and lichens. There is no better example of this particular style of gardening to be found anywhere in the British Isles.

173. ROUS LENCH COURT: ONE OF THE TERRACES LINKED BY STONE STEPS AND ENCLOSED BY TOPIARY

## 174. ST NICHOLAS: THE FORMAL GARDEN WITH GAY BEDS OF FLOWERS

**St Nicholas, Richmond, Yorkshire.** This is the garden of a great plantsman who has also the eye of an artist. The land slopes and has been divided into a series of terraces unequal in size and varying greatly in treatment. The old grey stone house dates back to Tudor times. Its walls are richly clothed with plants and a high buttressed wall which projects from it, enclosing a sheltered court, is similarly used as a protection for the exotic and often comparatively tender plants which astonishingly thrive in this Yorkshire garden. Near the forecourt of the house is a formal garden enclosed in shaped hedges of yew and at one point a great arch of yew leads to borders of shrubs, disposed in a more natural manner. This is in key with the main treatment which is informal with rough paths and steps winding through rock gardens, an old orchard bordered by ornamental shrubs and double herbaceous borders backed by hornbeam hedges for protection.

## 175. ST NICHOLAS: A HERBACEOUS BORDER BACKED BY A HORNBEAM HEDGE

**176. ST NICHOLAS: THE ROCK GARDEN WHICH IS OF SIMPLE CONSTRUCTION AND IS
GENEROUSLY PLANTED**

### 177. ST PAUL'S: THE LAWN FLANKED BY PLEACHED LIMES

**St Paul's Waldenbury, Hitchin, Hertfordshire.**
Garden making has been almost continuous at St Paul's
for more than two centuries, and it is today the
property of the Hon. David Bowes-Lyon, the President
of the Royal Horticultural Society who has made many
additions and improvements. The garden may be considered in four separate sections. Immediately around
the house are formal lawns and avenues of pleached
limes, the formal simplicity of the main design being
softened and elaborated by good planting, mainly of
roses, shrubs and herbaceous plants. At the far side of
the main lawn and centred on the north front of the
house is a great avenue cut through the woods which
cover the gently rising ground on this side. This avenue,
flanked by hedges of clipped beech, continues for nearly
half a mile and is terminated by a large statue of Hercules.
Other avenues radiate through the wood and there is also
a large clearing, terraced in grass and dominated by a
small temple. To the west of the house is a modern shrub
garden of informal design into which many herbaceous
and bulbous rooted plants have been successfully introduced. The fourth feature is an old monastery fish pond
below the woods through which the avenues are cut.
Weeping willows grow around it and a great bed of lupins
on its farther bank provides colour in early summer.

### 178. ST PAUL'S: THE TERRACED GARDEN IN THE WOOD

**179. ST PAUL'S: THE GREAT AVENUE TO THE NORTH OF THE HOUSE**

**180. ST PAUL'S: A RUINED ORANGERY NOW COVERED WITH FLOWERS**

**181. ST PAUL'S: WEEPING WILLOWS AROUND THE OLD MONASTERY FISH POND**

**182. ST PAUL'S: STEPS LEADING FROM THE LAWN TO THE LOWER TERRACE**

**183. SANDLING PARK: PRIMULAS AND RHODODENDRONS IN THE WOODLAND**

**Sandling Park, Hythe, Kent.** The original house was destroyed by bombs during the war and in its place Major and Mrs A. E. Hardy have built a severely plain but extremely well proportioned modern house in red brick. The garden around this is very simple, consisting of no more than a few flower beds and some climbing plants which serve to link the house with the beautiful parkland in which it stands. The main garden is some distance away and is made in a shallow and well-wooded valley. Here the beauty lies in the skill with which vistas have been contrived with the utmost care and yet with a complete illusion of artlessness.

Rhododendrons and azaleas, mostly of the hardier kinds, provide much of the colour though they are well supported by many other plants, notably great drifts of *Primula pulverulenta* in its various forms and masses of naturalised daffodils. The primulas have been planted in drainage ditches which were required in the wood to prevent the soil becoming too wet and stagnant for the rhododendrons. They enjoy the conditions so much that they have taken complete charge of these ditches, filling them so generously with self-sown seedlings each year that many have to be removed to prevent overcrowding. In addition to the native trees, many exotics or unusual species and varieties have been planted, some of which have made fine specimens. Particularly noteworthy is a huge and shapely fern-leaved beech and a well-developed incense cedar (*Libocedrus decurrens*).

184. SANDRINGHAM: THE DAIRY GARDEN, SO CALLED BECAUSE OF ITS GARDEN HOUSE BUILT LIKE A DAIRY

185. SANDRINGHAM: THE VERY EXTENSIVE ROCK AND WATER GARDEN IN WHICH PLANTING IS ON THE BOLDEST LINES

### 186. SANDRINGHAM: NATURALISED DAFFODILS IN THE PARK

**Sandringham, Norfolk.** The Norfolk house of the Queen was first purchased by the Prince Consort in 1861 as a home for the Prince of Wales (later King Edward VII). The garden as it is today is entirely the conception of successive royal owners and is notable for its spacious design and enormous herbaceous borders which lead right through the very extensive kitchen garden to an intimate enclosed garden, known as the Dairy Garden. The whole garden is divided into two quite separate parts by a public road which passes through the estate. The garden to the west of this road surrounds the house and is largely parkland with fine trees growing as single specimens or in groups and spinneys separated by lawns or cropped grass. There is, in addition, a large lake surrounded by a rock garden and an interesting series of formal gardens contained within two long rows of limes centres on the north end of the building which was the conception of King George VI and was designed for him by Mr Geoffrey Jellicoe. The garden to the east of the road is mainly devoted to vegetables and fruits, but it is here that the great herbaceous borders have been made and also the famous pergola which leads to these borders. It is conceived in the boldest terms, is very solidly constructed of masonry and timber and is well covered with a variety of climbing plants.

### 187. SANDRINGHAM: ONE OF THE GREAT HERBACEOUS BORDERS IN THE VEGETABLE GARDENS

**188. SCOTNEY CASTLE: THE PICTURESQUE RUINS SEEN ACROSS THE CASTLE MOAT**

**Scotney Castle, Lamberhurst, Kent.** The unique charm of the garden at Scotney Castle resides in the fact that in its midst are the remains of an ancient castle, a Tudor house and a ruined seventeenth-century mansion. These highly picturesque buildings stand on a tiny island surrounded by an unusually broad moat, the whole being set in delightful woodland well diversified with azaleas, rhododendrons and other exotic shrubs. These remnants of old dwellings are no longer inhabited, a new house of massive proportions having been built in 1837 of local stone on an eminence some distance away. The quarry from which this stone was hewn lies behind the house in the direction of the ruins and a balustraded terrace has been constructed on its rim. It is from this point

that one of the loveliest views is to be obtained, over the tree tops to the gleaming water and the romantic buildings which it protects.

There has been no need for the landscape gardener to use great art at Scotney as nature has done most of the work for him. Many of the trees are old and have reached the full beauty of maturity. Sufficient conifers have been included to give a satisfactory and often dramatic contrast to the broad leaved trees without producing a sombre effect. In addition, flowering shrubs and climbers have been planted around the ruins and in the moat there are many water lilies and other aquatics. The woodland is enriched with many exotic trees and is notable for its fine autumn colour.

**189. SCOTNEY CASTLE: REMNANTS OF THE ANCIENT CASTLE, TUDOR HOUSE AND SEVENTEENTH CENTURY MANSION**

**190. SCOTNEY CASTLE: THE WOODLAND AND RUINS SEEN FROM THE TERRACE ABOVE THE QUARRY**

**191. SEDGWICK PARK: ROCK AND WATER FEATURES OUTSIDE THE CENTRAL DESIGN**

**Sedgwick Park, Horsham, Sussex.** In this garden herbaceous plants and shrubs, so often associated with natural settings, have been employed to add colour and life to an essentially formal design. In outline this is an avenue of yew, neither continuous nor regular in width, but following a perfectly straight axis centred upon the terrace to the south of the house. At first the trim yew walls are low and square, bordered by lawns which are themselves broken by patterned beds of simple design. Quite suddenly, the design becomes more complex, the yew hedges twisting and circling to enclose a statue and flower beds. There is a sudden drop in the level of the garden and beyond this the hedges become higher and broken into deep buttresses like the wings of a stage, between which is a sheet of water filled with water lilies and surrounded by moisture-loving plants. Once again the enclosing hedges narrow and become simpler in form, concentrating the eye upon the distant view to the South Downs in the direction of Chanctonbury. To one side is a rock and water garden on more conventional lines; to the other a heather garden and shrub borders leading to an extensive woodland garden. Near the house are two rose gardens and some fine herbaceous borders.

**192. SEDGWICK PARK: ROSES AND FORMAL BEDS NEAR THE HOUSE**

**193. SEDGWICK PARK: THE CENTRAL WATER GARDEN ENCLOSED BY BUTTRESSED HEDGES OF YEW**

**194. SHEFFIELD PARK: THE HOUSE SEEN ACROSS THE FIRST LAKE**

**Sheffield Park, Fletching, Sussex.** This is a tree and shrub garden in the twentieth century manner but, unlike many such gardens, it has been most carefully and professionally planned for landscape effect. The house, which is in the late eighteenth-century Gothic style, stands on rising ground at the head of a broad, shallow valley. This has been dammed at four points to form a series of large lakes flanked by fine trees and shrubs which tend to exaggerate the depth of the valley and so improve the central vista across the water.

This planning is most effective and is greatly enhanced by the planting which is varied and good. Rhododendrons are used freely and also trees and shrubs which colour in the autumn, so that this garden, attractive throughout the season on account of the landscaping, has two peak periods of colour, one in May and June when the rhododendrons, kalmias and other shrubs are at their best, and the other in

October and November as the leaves turn scarlet and yellow prior to falling. Some of the rhododendrons are new seedlings raised at Sheffield Park and as these are mainly hybrids of the late-flowering *R. discolor*, the rhododendron season here continues well into June.

Bluebells, which, surprisingly, did not grow naturally in these woods, have been imported in tens of thousands to add their colour to the spring display and daffodils have also been naturalised in vast numbers. Gentians have been planted to give long rivers of intense blue, used deliberately to contrast with the red and coppery shades of autumn foliage.

Part of the woodland has been made a pinetum in which many fine and rare conifers have been established including the beautiful weeping *Picea Breweriana*, the spire-like *Picea Omorika* and rather tender *Pinus Montezumae*. Many of the trees have now reached maturity and, as they have been given ample space, are specimens of great beauty.

195. SHEFFIELD PARK: WHITE FLOWERED RHODODENDRONS GIVE A JUNGLE-LIKE ENCLOSURE TO THIS WOODLAND PATH

196. SHEFFIELD PARK: THE LAWN AND VIEW ACROSS THE HEAD OF THE VALLEY WITH GROUPS OF RHODODENDRONS

**197. SHRUBLANDS PARK: ONE OF THE CROSS AVENUES WHICH PUNCTUATE THE DESCENT**

**198. SHRUBLANDS PARK: THE HUGE PARTERRE AND LOGGIA SEEN FROM THE STONE STAIRCASE**

**199. SHRUBLANDS PARK: THE HOUSE AND STAIRCASE AS SEEN FROM THE LOGGIA**

**Shrublands Park, Coddenham, Suffolk.** This has been called an Italian garden in England and no more apt description could be found. It was designed in the mid-nineteenth century by Sir Charles Barry and it occupies the steep slope of a ridge of chalk overlooking flat country. On the summit of the hill stands the house, a massive Georgian structure with striking additions in the Italian style, and below this a great stone staircase of elaborate design descends the hillside in a series of flights, divides near the foot into a huge semi-circle partly enclosing a fountain basin, and so leads to a parterre of the noblest proportions enclosed by trees and with a columned loggia on its further side. An ornate archway at the head of the stairs frames the loggia below. Elsewhere plants enter more fully into the scheme, as in the transverse walk which cuts across the main axis beneath the escarpment and in the generous planting of the upper terrace.

### 200. SISSINGHURST CASTLE: THE SPRING GARDEN WITH PLEACHED LIMES

**Sissinghurst Castle, Cranbrook, Kent.** This castle is, in fact, only a fragment of a castle, yet in some respects it is all the more dramatic for that, its twin Tudor towers standing isolated in the peaceful Kentish countryside in a most unexpected and effective manner. Several oast houses cluster near it and two cottages stand within the grounds. These cottages, with some old pink brick walls left from the original building, tend to split up the ground so that this is, in fact, not so much one garden as a series of gardens, each intimate in design and intended to be viewed at some particular time of the year. Thus there is a coppice of old hazel bushes densely underplanted with polyanthus which is magnificent in early spring; twin borders flanked by pleached limes which have also been planted for spring effect; a walled garden of old roses, superb in colour and fragrance in early summer, and a 'white' garden which is at its best when the lilies are out in July.

### 201. SISSINGHURST CASTLE: POLYANTHUS NATURALISED IN A HAZEL COPPICE

**202. SISSINGHURST CASTLE: OLD-FASHIONED FLOWERS IN ONE OF THE NUMEROUS INTIMATE GARDENS WHICH ARE SKILFULLY STRUNG TOGETHER**

**203. SOUTH LODGE: DECIDUOUS AZALEAS MASSED BESIDE THE LAWN NEAR THE HOUSE**

**South Lodge, Lower Beeding, Sussex.** Only a few yards separate the entrance of South Lodge and Leonardslee and both gardens are in the natural style, yet, despite these points in common, they have little similarity. For one thing South Lodge lacks the dramatic contours of Leonardslee. The garden had to be made on comparatively level land though it falls to the south with fine views of the South Downs. It is, nevertheless, a more enclosed garden partly surrounded by tree screens beneath which rhododendrons and azaleas thrive. Indeed it is these azaleas which constitute one of South Lodge's main glories for they are mostly seedlings that have been raised there and they include some remarkably fine flowers. Wide lawns are broken by irregular plantings of trees and shrubs, denser and less formal the farther one gets from the house precincts. One part has been converted into a large rock and water garden in the conventional Edwardian manner and on the lower ground to the south there is a series of lakes. Many of the trees are of great interest and there is a notably fine specimen of the so-called handkerchief or ghost tree, *Davidia involucrata*.

**204. STOURHEAD: THE LAKE SO CAREFULLY PLANNED FOR ROMANTIC EFFECT**

**Stourhead, Mere, Wiltshire.** This is one of the most famous landscape gardens of the eighteenth century and certainly one of the best preserved, yet oddly enough it was not designed by any of the outstanding landscape gardeners of that period. Henry Hoare, who made it, was an amateur who has left a lasting memorial to his skill in the splendidly bold conception of Stourhead. The garden is made around one large lake and two smaller ones, all artificial, though one would scarcely guess this by looking at them. The Palladian mansion is well removed from this garden and plays no part in it, but there are several buildings, including a Temple of Flora and a Pantheon, which enter intimately into the design. Exotic plants, so dear to the twentieth-century gardener, there are practically none, the whole effect of well-wooded hill and dale being obtained with native trees and shrubs. Even the colour of this garden is mainly confined to that of leaf, branch and water diversified by the occasional firm white lines of well considered masonry. Today only the rather over elaborate grotto beside the main lake seems out of place though very typical of its period.

206. STOURHEAD:
A THIRD VIEW OF
THE LAKE SHOW-
ING THE SKILFUL
USE OF TREES TO
ACCENTUATE THE
NATURAL CON-
TOURS OF THE
LAND

## 207. SUTTON END: LAWN AND HARDY PLANT BORDERS BACKED BY TREES

**Sutton End, Petworth, Sussex.** Admirable use of shrubs, herbaceous plants and alpines is the feature of this medium size garden. Informality has been maintained without loss of design and everywhere one is conscious of a firm line underlying the free use of the rich planting material which is available to the present-day garden maker. Particularly interesting is the way in which the various types of plants have been combined into one harmonious whole, so that, for example, rock plants and dwarf shrubs flank the rough stone steps leading to an irregular lawn which is itself surrounded by herbaceous plants backed by shrubs and trees. Conifers and other evergreens are used to give solidity to the whole design. Dry walls provide a further excuse for liberal planting and there is an unusual and attractive use of a wall in front of the house to contain a sunken border reminiscent of a flower-planted ha-ha which permits an uninterrupted view from the house of the park beyond.

## 208. SUTTON END: THE GARDENER'S COTTAGE

## 209. SUTTON COURTENAY MANOR HOUSE: TOPIARY SPECIMENS GIVE EMPHASIS TO A GARDEN IN THE COTTAGE STYLE

**Sutton Courtenay Manor House, Berkshire.** It is fitting that this very old manor house should have a garden in the romantic English tradition. There is, at Sutton Courtenay, something of the cottage garden but on a much more elaborate and extended scale. There are closely packed flower beds filled with a marvellous patchwork of bloom which gains charm from its variety and somewhat haphazard arrangement. Point and emphasis is lent to the whole scheme by numerous topiary specimens, some simple in form, others clipped into strange shapes and the whole enclosed by well-grown hedges and flower decked walls. There is also a rose garden treated in the same free manner and similarly sheltered by wall and hedge beyond which the garden becomes progressively more informal as one proceeds towards the Thames, which is about 200 yards away from the house.

**210. TALBOT MANOR: WIDE GRASS PATHS WINDING BETWEEN EVEN WIDER BEDS PLANTED WITH SHRUBS AND WILD ROSES**

**Talbot Manor, Fincham, Norfolk.** This is a plantsman's garden which has been designed with unusual care and has an added interest in that it has been made in a part of the country usually considered too cold for many of the exotic shrubs and herbaceous plants which, in fact, thrive remarkably well at Talbot Manor. The garden may be considered in five main sections. First, around the house, there is a garden of simple design with lawns, beds and a high wall which has been used to give shelter to a number of remarkable but rather tender shrubs. Beyond this is a larger and more elaborate garden backed by a fine hedge of copper beech. The land is flat and has to be drained, so full use has been made of the drainage ditches to grow a great variety of moisture-loving plants. The ditches also feed a water and bog garden, the whole development in this section being on 'natural' lines. Beyond the beech hedge is a still larger area known as Four Acres. Here the treatment is open and spacious, large, irregularly shaped beds of shrubs being separated by wide areas of lawn. Trees give added height and variety but there are not so many as to give any sense of enclosure. By contrast the small arboretum which adjoins Four Acres is heavily planted and contains an exceptionally wide variety of trees. At one corner the land is particularly damp and here a collection of willows has been made. The fifth, and in some ways the most important, feature of Talbot Manor, is the range of green-houses in which a great number of rare tropical plants are grown.

**211. TALBOT MANOR: THE ROCK GARDEN WITH MOISTURE-LOVING PLANTS BEYOND.
DRAINAGE DITCHES PROVIDE WATER**

**212. THORNBURY CASTLE: ELEMENTS OF THE TUDOR GARDEN DESIGN CAN STILL BE SEEN**

**Thornbury Castle, Thornbury, Gloucestershire.** The garden at Thornbury Castle was first made in early Tudor times and, though it has since seen many vicissitudes and changes, some elements of Tudor design are still to be found in it. Gone are many of the elaborations of earlier days, but the formal pattern remains, grass plots replacing many of the beds which, no doubt, once occupied the site. There are also the finely grown and well cut hedges that give that sense of enclosure so dear to the sixteenth century gardener—not, of course, the original hedges, but hedges, one may feel, of similar character to those that first guarded the flower beds within. An account of the garden, written in 1521 by the commissioners of Henry VIII, speaks of a 'goodly gardeyn to walk ynne, closed with high walles imbattled' and that might well serve as a description of Thornbury Castle garden today.

### 213. TINTINHULL HOUSE: FORMAL DESIGN AND INFORMAL PLANTING

**Tintinhull House, near Yeovil, Somerset.** The west front is a lovely example of eighteenth century architecture and, in recent years, it has been given a garden which, while perfectly in keeping with it, yet provides scope for the cultivation of a great many of the shrubs and other hardy plants that are now popular. Moreover it is a labour-saving garden and one in which great attention has been paid to the skilful use of colour. The main portion of the garden is long in proportion to its width and a virtue has been made of this by designing it in several quite distinct sections strung along a path which is itself centred on the west front of the house. In this manner the maximum effect has been obtained from the vista either viewed towards or away from the house and at the same time a series of incidents has been provided which can only be seen by moving along the path. The first of the small gardens is nearly enclosed by brick walls which date from the erection of the west facade and are perfectly in keeping with it. These walls have been well planted and serve to tie the house into the garden scheme. Clipped shrubs accent the line of the path. The last garden has a formal circular pool which recaptures the architectural style of the house and a further rectangular garden, set at right angles to the main axis, also contains a long pool and is terminated by a stone built loggia.

### 214. TINTINHULL HOUSE: THE CENTRAL PATH AND LILY POOL

**215. TINTINHULL HOUSE: TWO SECTIONS OF THE GARDEN AS SEEN FROM THE HOUSE**

**216. TRESCO ABBEY:
PALMS FLANKING A
STONE STAIRCASE**

**217. TRESCO ABBEY:
ONE OF THE HILLSIDE
WALKS LEADING
BETWEEN RARE
EXOTIC PLANTS**

**218. TRESCO ABBEY:
ANOTHER VIEW OF
THE HILLSIDE WITH
THE PERGOLA ON
WHICH STRANGE
SUCCULENTS GROW**

**219. TRESCO ABBEY: THE ABBEY SEEN ACROSS THE LAKE**

**Tresco Abbey, Tresco, Isles of Scilly.** Tresco, like its sister isles, obtains the full benefit of the warm Gulf Stream, and seldom knows the rigours of frost. But equally it is exposed to the unrestrained violence of Atlantic gales which have deterred most Scilly islanders from planting trees and have led them to protect their bulb fields with hedges of euonymus, pittosporum and other wind-resistant shrubs. Not so Augustus Smith who began to live at Tresco Abbey in 1843 and, soon after determining to make a collection of rare and semi-tender plants, prepared for this venture by encircling the site of his proposed garden with a massive windbreak of cupressus and pine. Within this shelter belt his dream has been realised and today the garden at Tresco Abbey resembles those of the French Riviera in its luxuriance of palms and cycads, cacti, giant agaves, aloes and other succulents. The blue African lily (agapanthus) and the New Zealand flax (phormium) have become so firmly established that they have strayed far out into the sand dunes beyond the garden. Mesembryanthemums cover the walls and rocks with their vividly coloured flowers. The fragrant genista (*Cytisus racemosus*), which in most English gardens must be grown as a pot plant in the greenhouse, here forms great bushes in the open and the giant echiums of Mexico rear their massive blue spires.

**220. TRESCO ABBEY: NATURAL ROCK WORK ON THE HILLSIDE**

**221. UPTON HOUSE: THE VEGETABLE, FRUIT AND FLOWER GARDENS AND LAKE**

**Upton House, Edgehill, Warwickshire.** The house stands on a plateau only a little distance from a valley so steep sided and sudden in its descent that hint of its existence can be obtained only from the house itself. From this point, looking south, all one is aware of are some formal stone terraces connecting the lovely honey coloured building with an ample expanse of lawn. Only on crossing this lawn and look-down into the valley does one become aware of a whole series of gardens below and of a long narrow lake which appears like a river in the bottom of the valley. The first and steepest slopes are thickly planted with a medley of flowers but farther down the central portion is almost entirely devoted to a large kitchen garden. On either side of this paths lead down to the waters edge, that to the east being flanked by double borders of herbaceous plants and that to the west passing by two enclosed gardens sheltered by yew hedges.

From the far side of the valley an almost bird's-eye impression is obtained of the garden so steep is the opposite slope. From here it can be seen how well the kitchen garden fits into the scheme and how the belt of trees beyond the house completes the picture.

**222. UPTON HOUSE: DOUBLE HERBACEOUS BORDERS LEADING TO THE LAKE**

**223. WAKEHURST PLACE: AZALEAS, MAPLES AND OTHER CHOICE TREES AND SHRUBS**

**Wakehurst Place, Ardingly, Sussex.** One of the most notable collections of trees and shrubs to be found anywhere in England has been made in this garden, admirably situated on a narrow ridge of land between two valleys the steep sides of which afford splendid air drainage and so protect the garden from many of the worst spring frosts. The house itself is a grey stone Elizabethan mansion. The garden immediately around it is simple, well kept lawns sweeping right up to the south front and allowing its architectural beauties to be fully revealed. This conventional planning soon gives way to an informal and somewhat intricate arrangement of borders separated by winding grass paths or larger stretches of lawn. These borders are filled with shrubs, the planting in some cases being so close that the surface of the soil is completely concealed by the thicket of growth. To achieve this result many shrubs of compact, dense habit have been used, such as

heathers and evergreen azaleas together with some rock plants.

There are several large lakes, each of which has been treated differently. On the banks of one an extensive rock garden has been built; another is margined by moisture-loving plants and is nearly surrounded by fine trees; a third is more severe, a dark, still pool in the woodland and the fourth and largest serves to link the outermost parts of the woodland garden with the surrounding landscape. The extensive woodlands are themselves well underplanted with rhododendrons and other shade-loving shrubs which provide a natural and logical extension of the main garden.

From the house a long vista has been created towards the woodland and one of the lakes. A broad path passes between massed trees and shrubs and then descends into a long sunken garden the sides of which are thickly planted with azaleas, Japanese maples, magnolias and other shrubs.

**224. WAKEHURST PLACE: ONE OF THE WOODLAND LAKES LOOKING TOWARDS THE SUNKEN GARDEN**

**225. WAKEHURST PLACE: SHRUBS PLANTED TO GIVE COMPLETE GROUND COVER**

**226. WAKEHURST PLACE: THE LAKE AND ROCK GARDEN**

**227. WESTBURY COURT: THE STRAIGHT CANAL WITH THE T-SHAPED CANAL TO THE RIGHT**

**Westbury Court, Westbury-on-Severn, Gloucestershire.** Here is a water garden in the style beloved by the formal garden makers of the early eighteenth century. The water is used in two parallel canals, one perfectly straight, the other in the form of an elongated T. The first, or Long Canal, is centred upon a tall and elegant pavilion which once occupied an isolated position but is now connected with the house. The view from this pavilion is uninterrupted along the canal, through a clairvoyée left for that purpose in the boundary wall and so across the high road to the countryside beyond. Similarly the central axis of the T canal is also set upon a clairvoyée which greatly increases the sense of spaciousness in the vista so created. Brick pavilions flank the arms of the T canal and hedges of yew emphasise the formality of both canals. The wall which separates the garden from the road is continued around part of the head of the T canal so forming an enclosed garden which is the most profusely planted part of Westbury Court. At the head of this canal is a stone statue of Neptune. The two long canals are separated by a level lawn broken only by a few small flower beds so that everywhere the emphasis is on pattern rather than on elevation contrasted with the fine trees which encircle the garden. There are few better examples of this particular style of gardening to be found anywhere in the country.

**228. WESTBURY COURT: THE T-SHAPED CANAL SEEN FROM THE HEAD**

**229. WESTBURY COURT: FLOWER BORDERS AT THE HEAD OF THE T-SHAPED CANAL**

## 230. WESTONBIRT ARBORETUM: A GROUP OF INCENSE CEDARS AND PARROTIAS

**Westonbirt, Tetbury, Gloucestershire.** This is the most famous privately planted arboretum in the British Isles and it deserves its reputation. The arboretum is, in fact, in two quite separate parts, the older and more carefully planned being in sight of Westonbirt House and the newer further afield and intended primarily as a collection of trees and shrubs rather than as a setting for a mansion. In both cases, however, the general policy of planning is the same; very wide 'rides' of roughly mown grass between large blocks of trees underplanted with shrubs. It is in the grouping of the plant material itself rather than in the basic elements of design that this arboretum reflects the genius of its creator, Sir George Holford. A notable example of this is to be found in the extraordinarily bold grouping of the column-like and dark green *Libocedrus decurrens* flanked by the low, spreading growth of *Parrotia persica*, the leaves of which turn a brilliant yellow in autumn. There are many examples of such skilful grouping at Westonbirt.

**231. WILTON HOUSE: THE FORMAL GARDEN IN ITALIAN STYLE ALONGSIDE THE HOUSE**

**Wilton House, Salisbury, Wiltshire.** This garden has been described as the first of the landscape gardens in England for it was started as early as 1732 by the ninth Earl of Pembroke and William Kent. To make room for the sweeping park which they designed it was necessary to remove in its entirety an elaborate Renaissance garden of formal parterres. No change could have been more drastic for in place of the geometric beds and clipped shrubs of the French garden, appeared a great area of grassland, broken by specimen trees and with a small hill in the distance surmounted by a triumphal arch. Not far from the house the small River Nadder flows through the grounds. This was widened to make a more imposing stream and was spanned by a magnificent Palladian bridge which thus became the principal architectural feature in the garden. Early in the nineteenth century a new formal garden in the Italian style was made to the west of the house, and this was renovated and improved during the present century and is now largely a rose garden.

**232. WILTON HOUSE: THE PALLADIAN BRIDGE ACROSS THE WIDENED RIVER**

**233. WILTON HOUSE: THE HOUSE SEEN FROM THE RIVER WITH THE FORMAL GARDEN TO THE LEFT**

## 234. WREST PARK: INFORMAL PLANTING OF FINE TREES

**Wrest Park, Silsoe, Bedfordshire.** The gardens at Wrest Park have seen many changes and, indeed, the mansion itself is the third to have stood on this site. Today the great house is used to house a research station, but much of the garden remains and particularly the great formal canal and avenues which were created in the Italian style. Here there was ample space to plan on the grand scale and the result has justified the work. These gardens were designed by the first Earl of Grey from about 1836 onwards. Statuary and buildings in the classical style play an important part and the whole is planned to give vistas of great length down formal avenues of clipped trees terminated in the case of the main avenue by the canal with its rather elaborate stone pavilion. The complicated bedding schemes of earlier years can no longer be carried out but the basic design remains the same.

## 235. WREST PARK: THE AVENUE LEADING TO CANAL AND PAVILION